COMING OUT IN FAITH

Coming Out in Faith

Voices of
LGBTQ Unitarian Universalists

Susan A. Gore and Keith Kron, Editors

SKINNER HOUSE BOOKS

BOSTON

Printed in the United States

Cover and text design by Suzanne Morgan

print ISBN: 978-1-55896-619-2
eBook ISBN: 978-1-55896-620-8

6 5 4 3 2 1
14 13 12 11

Library of Congress Cataloging-in-Publication Data

Coming out in faith : voices of LGBTQ Unitarian Universalists / Susan A. Gore and Keith Kron, editors.

    p. cm.

 Includes bibliographical references.

  ISBN 978-1-55896-619-2 (pbk.:alk. paper)—ISBN 978-1-55896-620-8

(ebook)

 1. Unitarian Universalist sexual minorities—Religious life. I. Gore, Susan A. II. Kron, Keith.

 BX9867.C66 2011

 289.1'320866—dc22

                     2011007043

CONTENTS

Introduction

What does it mean to live in a society with deeply embedded expectations about heterosexuality and gender identity, knowing they don't fit you in some important way? How do you navigate the assumption that you cannot be lesbian, gay, bisexual, transgender, and/or queer—and spiritual or a person of faith?

Our goal in creating this collection of personal stories was to give voice to both the uniqueness of and the commonalities shared by LGBTQ people of faith. We tried to be inclusive as we approached clergy and laity ranging in age, color, geographic locale, physical ability, and economic background. The responses we received were remarkable.

The authors included here identify as Unitarian Universalist; however, all but two grew up in mainstream religious traditions that still regard homosexuality as unnatural, inherently disordered, and incompatible with church teaching. In contrast, in 1970 the Unitarian Universalist Association General Assembly approved the first of several resolutions affirming "the inherent worth and dignity" of lesbians, gay men, bisexual people, and, since 2007, people who are transgender.

We posed three questions to each person we invited to share their story:

- How has Unitarian Universalism affected your life as an LGBTQ person?
- How do Unitarian Universalist churches still struggle with understanding the lives of their LGBTQ members and LGBTQ issues beyond the sanctuary or minister's office?
- How do you take your faith into the wider world as an LGBTQ person?

The stories we received are filled with joy in response to the first question. "Coming home," "feeling whole," and similar metaphors appear in every one of these fifteen essays. The same stories also illustrate, sometimes with painful clarity, how far we still have to go, individually and as a faith. Unlearning any oppression is not a checklist but a process, often needing some grace along the way.

Being different in a culture based on the presumption of heterosexuality and mutually exclusive norms of masculinity and femininity is hard work. Granting there are exceptions, LGBTQ identity is invisible unless we choose to come out. The calculus of to whom, when, and how much is constantly engaged. Coming out also shifts how we are seen. Our sexual/gender identities almost always dominate the way "straight" people perceive us, overriding other qualities we may feel are equally or more important, such as our personal ethics or community contributions, or whether we are good daughters, sons, parents—or citizens. Dual expectations exist within the so-called gay community as well. Many gay men and lesbians regard bisexual people as outsiders. Perceptions are also complicated by the dilemmas of naming. Language surrounding transgender identity, in particular, is far from codified.

Robert Frost wrote that, in a book containing twenty-four poems, the book itself is the twenty-fifth. So it is with this collection of essays. They are ordered chronologically, from our oldest contributors to our youngest, ranging from eighty to seventeen. The people's history told in this set of stories—partial accounts though they may be—chronicles the awakening of LGBTQ collective consciousness into a civil rights movement that defies either/or categorization.

Why is it important to point out the richness of connections across differences that society prefers to enforce as boundaries? As Nigerian author Chimanamanda Adichie writes,

> The consequence of a single story is this: It robs people of dignity. It makes recognition of our equal humanity difficult. It emphasizes how we are different rather than how we are similar. When we reject the single story, when we realize there is never a

single story about any place, we regain a kind of paradise.

Our fiercest hope is that this collection will serve as a catalyst for others to share their stories with their friends, families, and faith communities, celebrating how far we have come and giving hope for how far we can go, in faith.

—Susan A. Gore and Keith Kron

A NOTE ON LANGUAGE

Language is personal and powerful, especially for those whose identities have been marginalized as outside the cultural mainstream. One result reflected in this collection is that authors use different terms to describe their primary identities. You will see the terms *gay*, *lesbian*, *bisexual*, *transgender*, *queer*, *genderqueer*, and sometimes multiple terms together to identify one's orientation and/or gender. We have chosen to embrace this rich diversity of language and honor contributors' choices rather than impose "standard" language.

People who identify as queer, transgender, or genderqueer illustrate the growing edge of changing language. Until recently, for example, the term *queer* was viewed within the LGBT community strictly as an epithet, a verbal attack that might well precede physical abuse. Many, though by no means all, gay youth have reclaimed *queer* as a badge of pride. Some use it as a term of endearment.

Similarly, some people who identify as transgender reject gender-specific pronouns—*he, she, him, her*—in favor of gender-neutral terms such as *ghe, gher,* and *hir.* The fact that authors within this collection choose different pronouns highlights just how fluid language can be.

It is worth noting that there are people who are in same-sex relationships or who identify as LGBTQ privately who do not want to be described by any particular label. It is also important to remember that sexual orientation and gender identity are distinctly different dimensions of identity. Someone may be transgender and gay, lesbian, bisexual, straight, or asexual.

Unfortunately, the sheer number of terms and usages related to LGBTQ people can lead to self-defensive withdrawal into silence "for fear of offending" or an aggressive response that these self-descriptive labels reflect nothing more than attempts to shock and/or confuse. We forget how many different ways people describe themselves and each other based on the situation and their level of intimacy. In general, we think nothing of the complexity of choosing whether to use someone's first name, first and last name, married name, professional title, parental status, geographic origin, age, race, or nationality to identify them. We do this based on circumstances and social conventions.

The key to navigating appropriate terminology relating to LGBTQ individuals or groups is essentially the same. Listening to how people refer to themselves is a great start, although not a sure bet. For example, you don't want to appropriate language that people who are LGBTQ may use based on their shared identities. When in doubt, asking the open-ended question, "How do you prefer to be addressed?" usually leads to a simple response: "I prefer . . . " If you are open to it, your query may provide an opportunity for dialogue about the meaning of someone's self-description. Either way, asking in a way that demonstrates respect is likely to elicit appreciation for your attempt to avoid operating on the basis of assumptions.

The variety of identities in what was once known simply as the "gay" community has expanded exponentially. Acronyms that reflect the growing awareness of diversity within the community now include a variety of shorthand combinations of the following letters:

A (for ally)	L (for lesbian)
B (for bisexual)	T (for transgender)
G (for gay)	Q (for queer)
I (for intersex)	Q (for questioning)

LGBT tends to be the most frequent abbreviation of this sort at present. We have chosen to use LGBTQ when speaking in our own voices to include the empowerment connotation of the word *queer* and because *queer* describes any orientation or identity that does not conform to societal norms.

First, last, and always, terminology is never as important as honest and respectful intent. Be patient with yourself and your dialogue partner. Silence is the most powerful enemy of understanding. Keep talking, and keep listening, even when you're not sure of the words.

Breaking Through at Midlife

Ed Kobee and Al Usack

ED: I grew up happily in a blue-collar neighborhood in Buffalo, New York. Our family attended the South Park American Lutheran Church. I was really a true believer until about halfway through my teens, when reason finally yanked me from the comforting feelings that true believership bestows. I discovered Unitarian Universalism after college, and although I had vowed never to join an organized religious movement again, I started occasionally attending the Paint Branch Unitarian congregation outside Washington, D.C., in 1958. However, another five years passed before I felt comfortable enough to sign the membership book, probably because of my blue-collar background.

During my early teens, I discovered that I enjoyed having sex with other guys my own age. I never admitted that I was doing something abnormal, because we all believed we would meet the right girl, fall in love, and raise a family. I never even heard there was such a thing as a gay community, much less that I should be a member of such a thing. But as time moved on, I started to worry that I would never find a woman who turned me on, so I started dating. During my heterosexual encounters, I often fantasized about having sex with men.

AL: From the time I was quite young, I had trouble with my sexuality. I grew up on a farm in rural Wisconsin in the thirties and forties. Until I graduated from high school, I never heard of homosexuality and what that meant. I had crushes on girls but always held back. I did like to dance, though, and there was no option other than dancing with girls. I was always curious about boys who had steady girlfriends. And I was curious about boys and sex, especially in the locker room before and after basketball games. All in all, I tried to be like my three older brothers and was active in sports. I was on the high school baseball and basketball teams, and played touch football with my pals. However, although I loved sports and still do, I was never very good at anything except being able to run fast.

In college, some girls tried to tempt me, but I continued to hold back. I had a lot of male friends, and we played ball and cards together and goofed off a lot, but I did not feel any sexual tension in these relationships. In my junior year, I became involved in theater and met a number of folks who were rumored to be "funny." I found both groups to be great fun, but as far as I can remember, I never felt that anyone tried to make a move on me.

ED: Like most of the men of my generation, I wanted marriage and a family. I married Louise in my late twenties. We had two wonderful children in the first three years. The marriage was rocky almost from the start, but we tried for ten years to make it work before divorcing. I received full custody of our children, ages seven and nine.

I had not had sexual relations with men, or other women, during my marriage. A year after the divorce, I started dating a wonderful woman, Cathy. Everything seemed to be right for us to marry, but I just couldn't make the commitment.

Cathy and I decided to take a human potential training called LifeSpring to see if we could understand ourselves better and, perhaps, smooth the path to marriage. At the end of the second LifeSpring training, I woke up in the middle of the night with a *eureka!* moment: I couldn't commit to marriage because I still wanted to have sex with men! When I shared this insight with Cathy, she insisted that I needed to resolve the issue before we moved on to marriage. She encouraged me to play out my fantasies about male sex, expecting, of course, that I would fulfill some teenage fantasies and realize I truly wanted a long-term relationship with her. Cathy even bought me my first pair of tight jeans and pushed me out of the house on Friday nights to go to the bars.

AL: A year after graduating from college, I was drafted into the Army, where I spent most of my career working at the

Pentagon. I began to date a girl from my hometown and asked her to marry me—the thing all young men did! After several months of engagement, she sent my ring back. I was crushed. Later, I realized that she was pretty smart, because marriage would never have worked out.

During this time, I also looked up a fellow from my college, then living in D.C., who was rumored to be homosexual. He invited me to a cabin his family owned, to help paint it. I accepted, hoping that I might be seduced. But nothing came of the weekend except my disappointment.

ED: At forty-two, I was really scared to start roaming gay bars. My entire vision of the gay community was shaped by one scene from the movie *Advise and Consent*, in which a senator is blackmailed by a man with whom he had had a sexual relationship many years before. While trying to search out the blackmailer, the senator finds himself in a dingy, overcrowded, smoky gay bar, where men are having sex. He eventually commits suicide. I remember thinking when saw the movie, "Thank God, I'm not like that!" Now, though, I was about to enter what looked like a nightmarish world that cherished youth and good looks over anything else. But I did muster up my courage and eventually entered my first gay bar—after walking around the block about half a dozen times. And so the adventure began.

AL: When I got out of the Army, I went back to school at the University of Wisconsin. I washed dishes and occasionally worked in the dining room, where Lola waited tables. I met her at a picnic for waitresses and bus boys at her dorm. Lola majored in social work, and we found we had a lot in common and enjoyed each other's company. We got married shortly after I graduated, at a very small ceremony in Washington, D.C. I had just begun working as a Central Intelligence Agency analyst.

After several years, Lola became pregnant with the first of our three daughters. We decided that we needed to find a church for our children to grow up in. I was basically unchurched. My dad thought that the greatest hypocrites sat in the front row at churches, so he refused to attend. My mother had been a Lutheran and volunteered at our local nondenominational church but never went to the Sunday services. When we were children, my parents sent me and my brothers and sister to a Sunday school conducted by a local farmer and part-time minister. We had to walk about a mile, and I hated to go, especially during the cold winters of northern Wisconsin.

Lola disdained the fundamentalist church that she had grown up in and I had no church background, so with our liberal religious leanings, we decided that a Unitarian church would be fitting. The first we attended was nearby All Souls Church Unitarian in D.C. We liked the church, and when we moved to Virginia in 1960, we went to the Fairfax Unitarian Church, which was then meeting in a local school.

ED: Cathy's plan to cure me of my fantasies didn't turn out as she had hoped. To my surprise and hers, I discovered that part of me which I had suppressed for so many years. For the first time in my life, my sex life and my emotional life came together with explosive force. I wanted to yell to the world "I am gay!" The feeling of euphoria was unbelievable.

I had enough sense to turn to my minister for advice. Well aware of my responsibilities, he cautioned me to go slowly into this new world—but added that he did not know much about gayness and the gay community. He referred me to Rev. Frank Robertson (himself a gay man) of All Souls Church Unitarian. Frank was very helpful to me, making me realize that there was a positive side to being gay and a positive side to being in the gay community. This was back in 1978, well before other Unitarian Universalist churches in the D.C. area had adopted gay-positive attitudes. Frank not only counseled gay folks but held ceremonies of union in the All Souls garden. Frank and his partner held monthly potluck dinners for the gay community at their home for several years before he was dismissed by All Souls Church for spending too much time on gay and lesbian issues. Frank also urged that I attend a conference of gay, lesbian, and bisexual persons in Norfolk. At that conference, I first encountered a really positive group of gay folk, enjoying a full life without the angst and game playing that went on in the bars.

AL: At first, Lola and I were not involved much in church activities. Then our minister, Rudy Nemser, had the bright idea to ask me to be on the Canvass Committee. I soon found out that church was much more than attending on Sundays and giving $100 per year. From then on, we got more and more involved, and the church soon became the center of our lives. In the 1970s, we became involved in a Unitarian Universalist program that set up groups of randomly selected individuals and families who would support each other, socialize, and participate in church activities, like an extended family. Rudy Nemser left our church, and when a search committee was selected to find a new minister, four members of our extended family, including myself, were elected. These groups were so popular that the other three members of the committee were in another extended family. Through this search process, I really began to develop a Unitarian Universalist spiritual outlook. After we selected a minister, I was elected to the church board and became president a couple of years later.

In the meantime, I was involved in local politics in Herndon, Virginia, where we lived, through my membership and activities with the Junior Chamber of Commerce chapter. In the early 1960s, I began experimenting sexually with men, especially while traveling to D.C. to take courses required for my work at the CIA. This experimentation progressed over the years. The forbidden fruit was exhilarating, but I felt a lot of guilt in my family relationships. I was so deeply in the closet that I even avoided the few folks who had come out in our congregation in fear that I would be suspected if I befriended them.

For many years, I went regularly to the Southeast Unitarian Universalist Summer Institute (SUUSI). SUUSI is a week-long program that meets at a university in southwest Virginia each year and provides a variety of workshops and activities for individuals and families. I usually went to SUUSI on my own, but in 1986, Lola went with me. We attended a wonderful course on the meaning of love. One of the sessions was on honesty and another was on not harming the one you love. Filled with self-loathing about my sexual exploits, I finally decided to take some steps to be more open with Lola. This was during the early years of the AIDS crisis, and I was having unprotected sex with men. I had been in Hong Kong for the first couple of years of the crisis, and AIDS was only rarely reported there, but when I got back to the United States in 1985, it was widespread. I went to a private urologist to be tested for HIV. The test was positive, and at that point, I came out to Lola. Although the test turned out to be a false positive, coming out to Lola was one of the most important things I ever did for both of us.

After much discussion, Lola and I agreed to go to joint and individual therapy to see if we could work things out. I had a therapist who did not understand gay people at all and was of no help to me. However, I found a support group, and the sharing of stories and support in the group was very helpful. I also found some support in the local Metropolitan Community Church, which was meeting in the Fairfax congregation's new building. Under the guise of concern for social justice, I went to a couple of their services. About the same time, I went to a meeting of an organization that had been founded in 1971 called the Unitarian Universalist Gay Caucus (now Interweave), at the Unitarian Universalist Association's (UUA) annual General Assembly in Rochester, New York. Much to my surprise, I found out that the UUA was quite supportive of LGBT folks.

ED: For nine years after I went to the Southeastern Conference, I managed balancing work, raising a family, being active at church, and going through three serious gay relationships. I came out to my children about a year after I started my journey into gay life. My daughter reacted positively to this revelation and my son negatively. It was several years before my son accepted me as a gay man. I volunteered at the Baltimore Gay Clinic as a receptionist and administrative assistant. This bit of volunteerism probably saved my life. The clinic staff became aware early on that there were some mysterious diseases that seemed to be connected to gay sexual activity. This was before these diseases were tied together as the complications of AIDS. I quickly modified my behavior, cutting way back on anonymous sex. Unfortunately, many of my friends from the Gay Married Men's Association and Gay Fathers of D.C. continued to participate in anonymous sex, using the commercial bathhouses as their primary sexual outlet. As a result, very many of my friends died in the AIDS epidemic. It hurts to think back on those memories.

In 1985, I suffered a tragedy that still causes me anguish: My lovely daughter, nineteen years old, beautiful, intelligent, vivacious, and well loved by all, was killed in a traffic accident. I shall never forget the love and support shown to me during this dreadful time by my Unitarian Universalist congregation, and especially by my minister, Rev. Ric Kelley.

I had become increasingly involved at church—singing in the choir, chairing a number of committees, and eventually becoming board chair in 1987. In the nine years since I had come out, I had not heard one word about gay, lesbian, or bisexual people from the pulpits of any of the churches in the D.C. area. Neither did I hear anything from the UUA in support of LGB issues. As board chair, I decided to go to my first General Assembly to see if I could stir up some interest in supporting LGB issues.

To my utter amazement, I discovered that the UUA had been supportive of LGB issues since 1970. There just was nothing happening locally, at least in the D.C. area. Another big surprise was Unitarian Universalists for LGBT Concerns and the Office of Lesbian and Gay Concerns (a staff office of the UUA). They offered many very helpful workshops at GA, especially the one titled "Coming Out at an Advanced Age." I attended because I thought I could contribute to it, since I had come out at the age of forty-two. That's where I saw Al for the first time. During introductions, Al explained that he was trying to come out at age fifty-seven. He happened to be from Fairfax, Virginia, a forty-minute ride from where I lived, so I went over to say hello after the workshop. That was it! We've been together now for twenty-three years. We have celebrated our anniversary by attending nearly every GA since then—twenty-two in all.

AL: Lola was on a two-month assignment in Thailand for the CIA (I had retired) when I attended that General Assembly. When I met Ed, it was love at first sight, and we have been together ever since. After General Assembly, I went to SUUSI and got wonderful help from a men's support group. I'm afraid that I was a basket case, with a marriage falling apart and madly in love with a man for the first time. The support I got at SUUSI really made me appreciate how sensitive Unitarian Universalist straight men can be. When Lola came back from Thailand, I told her about Ed. She was adamant that she was not about to accept a three-way relationship, and we agreed on an amicable separation. For a short time, I lived with a friend and visited Ed in Maryland on a regular basis. In the fall of 1987, I moved in with him permanently. Lola and I continued to be friends over the years. At first, she blamed Ed for our breakup, but after several years of healing, she became a part of our extended family. When Lola died several years ago, I was at her bedside, along with our children. I also participated in a wonderful memorial service for her at the Unitarian

Universalist Church in Fairfax, where she continued to be a member after we parted.

ED & AL: Toward the end of the 1987 General Assembly, Rev. Jay Deacon met with us and one other man from D.C. and asked us to try to get our local area churches involved in supporting the March on Washington for gay and lesbian rights in November. We agreed. The minister of the Accotink church joined us, and the four of us visited about twenty of the D.C.-area church boards over the next few months, asking them to support the march and open their doors to house Unitarian Universalists coming from out of town. We were astounded by the reactions of many of the churches. They seemed to have no inkling about LGBT issues, nor any idea why their church should give us support. We received comments from several board members that startled us: "Why are you wasting our time on this? There are so many other social problems that need our attention"; "Why do you talk about homophobia? I was in the Army, and we were certainly not scared of those guys. We knew how to handle them." Apparently, these attitudes were shared by many Unitarian Universalists, enough so that the UUA developed the Welcoming Congregation Program to make members of congregations aware of the LGBT community's need for acceptance and support. A few churches did offer to house marchers and provide support in October. We became activists for gay causes in our church and elsewhere as a result.

ED: Before we started visiting the various church boards, I came out at a board meeting of my church. I was the board chair, and the church was embarking on a capital fund campaign to build a new sanctuary. I did not want my gayness to become an issue in the church. I left the meeting to let the board talk about the issue. When I was invited to return, they unanimously asked me to stay on as board chair and supported our efforts to get other churches involved in the March on Washington.

AL: Generally, members of my new congregation at Paint Branch accepted me with open arms. The fact that Ed was president of the congregation at the time, and that I rapidly got involved in various committees, may have had something to do with their acceptance. In the meantime, a straight male member of my old Fairfax congregation decided to have a male-only going away party for me. Apparently, this did not sit too well with some members there. Also, when I returned to my old church to seek help at the LGBT March on Washington, I found that I was greeted mostly by the women. Many of the men appeared to be uncomfortable in my presence.

In 1988, I decided to work as an AIDS Buddy at the Whitman Walker Clinic in the Washington area. I was surprised at the number of women in our Buddy group and how much they helped in this terrible crisis. Both of the Buddies I worked with were about forty years old. The first was Larry, who was from a Catholic background and into leather. He was very out, and Ed and I were a bit unnerved when he parked his car sporting all kinds of gay stickers in our middle-class, straight neighborhood. I frequently visited him in his apartment. One day when I went to visit him, the door was locked and a number of fliers were lying around. I contacted the landlady, and we found that he had committed suicide. I was shocked, even though he had told me he had the drugs needed to do it. After his death, his family took over and I was not contacted at all about funeral arrangements. A friend of his and I did prepare a panel for the AIDS Memorial Quilt in his memory. Suicide was common among AIDS patients at that time, and part of our training was a wonderful course on assisted suicide.

My second Buddy was an African-American man who bravely informed the police about drug dealers in a drug-infested area of D.C. When I visited him, I always felt a bit uneasy about being in the area. Willy taught me a lot about living in the face of adversity. Unfortunately, he was given an experimental medication that caused mental deterioration, and he died at a hospice shortly after I met him. I was the only white person at his memorial service, which was led by his ex-wife. His twelve-year-old daughter also spoke at the very powerful service.

About the same time, a very good friend of ours was sick with AIDS, and I helped his partner care for him. By 1990, I felt burned out and dropped out of the Buddy program.

ED & AL: After our experiences with the local Unitarian Universalist churches, we decided that something needed to be done to make them aware of the needs of their LGBT members and the LGBT community as a whole. We helped set up a local LGBT group that met at our church in Paint Branch, Maryland, once a month for many years. It had a specific program for each meeting. We also started a popular LGBT film series that ran for years and drew a number of straight people. Members of other local Unitarian Universalist churches also joined the group, which eventually became an Interweave chapter.

The Paint Branch congregation responded positively, and we held our first service on homophobia in January 1988. It was one of the most emotional services the church had ever seen. Al and I were in tears. Even five years later, a member of the congregation thanked us for doing that service.

In 1988, we attended our first annual Continental Interweave Convocation (CONVO) in Portland, Maine. We arrived a day late because a blizzard had dropped two feet of snow on Portland, closing all area airports. We were excited to see what other churches were doing and immediately became involved in Continental Interweave. Ed joined the Continental Interweave board, followed by Al.

The Paint Branch congregation gave overwhelming support for our hosting of the 1992 CONVO, which a record-setting two hundred people attended. Participants had thirty workshops to choose from. Jay Deacon's keynote address was perhaps the most stirring call to action that we have heard from any Unitarian Universalist minister. We rarely missed a CONVO from 1988 to 2003, and we still occasionally attend. Besides its wonderful homecoming feel, CONVO has always offered interesting, supportive workshops and outstanding speakers.

Our congregation also supported our founding of the Interfaith Fairness Coalition of Maryland (IFCM). Its mission is to foster a more positive attitude toward LGBT people in non–Unitarian Universalist congregations statewide. Initially, the organization was funded as a standing committee of our congregation, receiving two $10,000 matching grants from the UUA and several smaller grants from other organizations. With this money, we were able to organize workshops at other churches. We compiled a list of gay-friendly congregations that is maintained to this day.

Rev. John Manwell from the Baltimore congregation was a strong supporter of the IFCM's goals. For example, he and his wife, Rev. Phyllis Hubbell, conducted a ceremony of union on the steps of the Maryland state capitol one very cold Valentine's Day in 1996. Organized by their congregation, the IFCM, and the Maryland National Organization for Women, the ceremony dramatized the need for LGBT marriage equality. We attended, were moved by the ceremony, and froze. The IFCM still organizes several interfaith services a year in support of the LGBT community.

Early on, we attended a board meeting of the Joseph Priestley District, a formal group of sixty Unitarian Universalist churches in Maryland, Pennsylvania, Delaware, D.C., and Virginia, to see if we could get district-level support for the LGBT community. To our surprise, halfway through our presentation, the Board moved to create a standing LGBT Concerns Committee, which helped spread the Welcoming Congregation Program throughout the JPD district. We personally conducted services and workshops throughout the district to support the Welcoming Congregation Program.

We helped start the Joseph Priestley chapter of Interweave, which included LGBT Unitarian Universalists from congregations across the district. We were able to exchange ideas and socialize together through this organization. JPD Interweave also set up a film library that loaned LGBT films to congregations and, for many years, sponsored two weekend retreats a year.

The 1993 March on Washington for Equal LGBT Rights was very special to us. We both volunteered two days a week in the national office of the March in Washington, D.C. We had long thought the national LGBT rights movement had been neglecting the positive role that religious organizations could offer. We thought we could best demonstrate this role by somehow organizing Unitarian Universalists across the country to support the March. About fifteen volunteers in the D.C. area formed a committee to promote Unitarian Universalist participation. Much work was required, but eventually three thousand from across the country showed up for the March. Local volunteers arranged housing, hosted a reception Saturday night before the March, organized a special service on Sunday morning, drove people to the March, gave marchers Unitarian Universalist pennants to wave, and participated in the most wondrous display of support that could be imagined.

The entire UUA Board of Trustees showed up for the weekend. When the board members entered All Souls Church Unitarian in downtown D.C. on that Sunday morning, more than one thousand people stood cheering and applauding for at least five emotion-filled minutes. Then-UUA president Rev. Bill Shultz spoke, adding even more energy to the gathering. We left the service, got down to the March assembly area, and found that Unitarian Universalist–identified marchers far outnumbered those from any other religion, including the contingent from the primarily gay Metropolitan Community Church of North America. The next issue of the *UU World* magazine featured a cover photograph of Unitarian Universalist marchers carrying their signs and pennants. Not many events in one's life can equal the thrill and satisfaction we got from seeing this outpouring of support!

ED: In 1995, Al and I had our ceremony of union at the Paint Branch church, eight years after we became a couple. This time was very special for us, and for our families. We fussed and planned for several months, wanting so much to impress upon the mostly heterosexual attendees that the love we bore for each other was as real as that of a heterosexual couple. Three ministers participated, along with all four of our children, my two sisters, and a grandchild. Rev. Meg Riley's homily touched us deeply, as did the readings of Rev. Virginia Knowles and Rev. Rod Thompson. The choir sang "Love and Understanding," my favorite choir anthem. More than two hundred people attended, jamming the church to capacity. It was a wonderful testimony of support for the two of us, yet another gift from our congregation, and a moment to treasure for the rest of our lives.

AL: I continued to go to SUUSI almost every year in the eighties and nineties. I went by myself, because Ed thought that it should be my time to join the many friends I had met over the years. We had an active LGBT group at SUUSI,

with regular meetings, workshops, and a lot of socializing. I particularly remember the great dances there. We almost always had a dance for men only and one for women only, as well as a special dance celebrating acceptance of LGBT folks. Often, my friends and I danced as a group—some of us did some pretty innovative steps! I haven't been to SUUSI for a long time and sort of miss the many wonderful workshops and the great fun we had there.

ED & AL: Around the year 2000, we decided to move to a retirement community. We first looked in the Washington, D.C., area. It was expensive, but the bigger problem was that we did not feel we could be as openly gay as we wanted to be. Many of the people we talked to just did not understand our hesitation; they assumed automatic acceptance, but we found out through experience that this just wasn't so. Also, we realized that the gay people in these communities were mostly in the closet, so they probably would not want to socialize with us for fear they might be outed. Finally, we found a wonderful gay retirement community in Florida.

We shared many happy times with the LGBT Unitarian Universalist communities in the Washington area and the Joseph Priestley District: spiritually rewarding retreats, parties, workshops, potlucks galore, bull sessions, support groups, gay pride marches, and social action activities. We found our work to help spread the Welcoming Congregation program throughout the district especially rewarding.

When it came time to move to Florida in 2003, we received special recognition from the district, our congregation, our local Interweave chapter, and the IFCM. How wonderful to realize we have made a difference.

We vowed to slow down our church participation when we moved to Florida. We spent the first year visiting three Unitarian Universalist churches convenient to our home. The first time we walked into the Manatee Unitarian Universalist Fellowship, we were greeted warmly by name by a gay man who had participated in one of our workshops in New Jersey. Small world indeed!

At first, we thought we could just drop all of our LGBT activism when we became members of the Manatee fellowship. Who were we kidding? Although Manatee is a Welcoming Congregation, there is still much to do, and we have become involved in renewing the fellowship's Welcoming status. We find ourselves once again caught up in the church whirl, deriving much satisfaction from the shared responsibility of keeping a small fellowship a vibrant asset to its members and the community. Most of our church involvement is in other areas, however: social justice, finance, denominational affairs, stewardship, membership, choir, and so on. And this is as it should be. We feel justly proud of the gay community when we look around and see how many of us volunteer to be on or to lead boards and committees, to help the hungry, to work with immigrant workers, and to help others who are in need. There is still much to do, of course, especially in helping LGBT folks outside our church in their struggles to be accepted and loved—but we find that more and more, we lean on others to do more of the grassroots work and confine ourselves to mentoring and supporting the work that others do.

◄o►

ED KOBEE grew up in a factory neighborhood of Buffalo, New York. He spent his career as a weapons system analyst for the Federal Civil Service at the Naval Ordnance Laboratory outside Washington, D.C. At the same time, Ed raised a son and a daughter who were seven and nine when he and his wife divorced. Ed joined the Paint Branch Unitarian Universalist Church in 1958.

AL USACK grew up on a dairy farm in Wisconsin and graduated from River Falls College in 1948. He moved to the D.C. area in 1957 to work for the CIA, where his specialty was research on the Communist Chinese economy. He retired in 1987. Al has three daughters and several grandchildren from his marriage of twenty-seven years.

Ed and Al have each been recognized by Interweave: Unitarian Universalists for LGBT Concerns with the Mark DeWolfe Award for Outstanding Service, and their activism for the LGBTQ community has been reported on the front page of the *Washington Post*, as well as in the *Washington Blade* and the *Baltimore Gay Paper*.

Take Courage

Beth F. Coye

My life journey did not lead me to a Unitarian Universalist congregation until I was fifty-seven years old. Upon reflection, the journey thus far has included many experiences that would have been deeply enriched and changed by Unitarian Universalist roots, friends, and ministers.

The ship of my life has traveled far but often in turbulent waters and low visibility. When I was young, my parents and my corner of the world were intolerant of who I sensed I might be. My intuition about my sexuality was felt but not acknowledged. I lived the lie.

In my precollege days, boys were good friends but not boyfriends. Had I been honest with myself, I would have identified more clearly my sexual attraction to girls. I stifled those feelings, focusing instead on studies and sports. With my mother's guidance, and because of its reputation for scholarship and its magnificent New England campus, I chose a women's college, Wellesley. For my junior year, I transferred to UNC-Chapel Hill and UCLA, two coed colleges, to experience more social relations with the opposite sex. I pledged a sorority. I partied. I dated. No sexual sparks flew. I enjoyed men's company and energy but had no romantic interest in them. Returning to Wellesley my senior year, I delighted in my challenging courses and friendships with women, still unmindful of my sexual orientation.

My father was a career naval officer, and I felt predestined to a Navy career. In 1960, I entered the Navy. I fell in love with it and with another officer, a woman. The Navy was just right; so too was the officer, who eventually became my partner of seventeen years. Although I fought against it, falling in love with a woman was surprisingly natural. Being as clueless about homosexuality as most Americans in the sixties, I certainly did not give much thought to self-identifying as a "queer," as my mother referred to homosexuals back then.

I was terribly confused. Given what Americans, my family and friends, and the United States Navy thought about homosexuals, how could I love another woman? My emotional and physical selves, however, informed me that I was fortunate to have discovered my sexual being and to find my soul mate.

For years I was torn: The Navy's rules and regulations stated that I should resign if I were sexually involved with a person of the same sex, yet I remained blissfully in love with a special woman. To assuage this dilemma, I dated several male naval officers, hoping against reality that I might be bisexual and meet society's heterosexist precept part-way. For my partner, who had already come to a decision about her own sexuality, this dating game was clearly a raw deal. We separated as a result, although she remains my best friend.

A sleepless night after I accepted a marriage proposal from a fellow officer compelled me to confront my own sexuality. I was thirty-two.

At the time, no friend, family member, or religious faith helped me with the marriage decision. Raised a Protestant, I was unchurched during this time. My former partner was not stationed nearby. My best female officer friends, whose friendships I truly valued then and now, could not help me, because same-sex behavior violated Navy regulations.

The marriage proposal pressed me to decide between living the "normal" life of a Navy wife and mother and living the less-than-normal life of a female naval officer who would have to play the military's inane game of relinquishing one's integrity for false standards. Turning down the proposal, disregarding the desires of my parents, discounting society's mores, and disobeying the Navy's severe antihomosexual regulations continually taxed my peace of mind.

I drew comfort from my conscience. I knew that marrying a man, however wonderful he might be as a husband, would have been unfair to the man, to my family, and to me. Even if my country, my family, and my fellow officers all thought my sexuality was abnormal or wrong, I needed to be me. I relied upon the strength of my own character, my family upbringing, and the moral ethics that church and my beloved Wellesley had instilled in me.

My choice not to marry was right. Before my mother's death at ninety-five in 2007, I told her that her greatest gift to her three children was the gift of self-esteem, which had carried me through some turbulent, self-searching times. Today's changes in societal norms about sexual orientation as well as my own Unitarian Universalist spiritual faith would have greatly helped me work through any marriage decision making. Life would have been less agonizing, less lonely.

I got through the proposal crisis, but another storm was brewing. Despite challenging, exciting assignments and an outstanding professional record and reputation, my love for the Navy was waning: In 1965, as the top-rated of thirty-seven naval officers graduating from American University's School of International Service master's program, I felt for the first time the sting of discrimination. Instead of granting my choice of orders to teach at the U.S. Naval Academy or to work in the Pentagon's politico-military affairs office, possible billets offered to the top students in the class, the Navy ordered me to a mediocre job. This decision was made because of my gender.

At that moment of denial and gender discrimination, I knew I would do something about changing the Navy's policies toward women. My experience was what Jane Reilly later labeled the "click," an awakening of feminist consciousness. Reilly's article, "The Housewife's Moment of Truth," appeared in the premiere issue of *Ms. Magazine* in 1971.

Unequal opportunities for military women, including limited career paths, thwarted my ambitions. In the late sixties and early seventies, I was engaged in a demanding assignment at the Naval War College in Newport, Rhode Island, as well as an after-hours project that would help rectify the lack of opportunities offered to Navy women. I had been tapped by the Chief of Naval Personnel to author a study that would become a benchmark regarding the status of military women and a conceptual framework for opening up military women's opportunities as directed by the Secretary of Defense.

To be an outspoken feminist was unacceptable behavior to most members of the Navy, both male and female. Nonetheless, something about speaking up for those women who were more silent, more junior, more threatened, and less educated, motivated me to present a solid case for Navy women's equality to the admirals.

I recommended that a comprehensive study be initiated to reformulate "the raison d'être of women in the Navy in light of recent changes in society and in the Navy." Under the leadership of the Chief of Naval Operations, Admiral Bud Zumwalt, that's exactly what happened. Today, Navy women have achieved stellar heights unforeseen by the Navy WAVES (Women Accepted for Volunteer Emergency Service) of yesteryear.

Even though I wasn't a Unitarian Universalist at that time, I realize in retrospect that Unitarian Universalist Principles were embedded in my soul, driving me to work long hours and put up with being called the Navy's "flaming radical women's libber" by my male counterparts of all ranks. The work was about the first Principle, "the inherent worth and dignity of every person," and the second Principle, "justice, equity, and compassion in human relations." Condoning or forgiving the Navy's unjust personnel policies toward its women was not my style.

The goal of every line officer is to become a commanding officer. Despite a reputation as a vocal feminist, my career flourished, and on March 17, 1977, I took command of a new shore activity in San Diego. What a thrilling day! Even though it rained, the ceremony inside the auditorium went smoothly, my proud parents and family and friends beamed, flags decorated the auditorium, and the troops stood proudly in their dress whites.

To be one of the Navy's first female commanding officers was, and continues to be, a great honor. Although the road remained rocky, it was often exhilarating and always challenging. The primary personal obstacle to creating an inclusive atmosphere within the command was not lack of human resources or expertise but my sexual orientation. From years of training, education, and mentoring, I had the skills necessary to handle the challenges of command.

But my sexual orientation kept interfering with my job satisfaction and obstructing my dreams. During the two-

and-a-half-year command tour, I discharged at least eight young men and women "for cause of homosexuality." Each discharge tore at my heart. I was sending home young competent sailors again and again.

Almost two years into the assignment, I learned that my commander, suspicious of my living with two other women, wished to force me out of command. He had put a tail on me for several weeks to prove his suspicion. Fear and a sense of betrayal rushed through me. After this breach of trust, the discharge of two young lesbians was a turning point for me, a second type of click. One might say this started the awakening of my LGBT consciousness, and led to my moment of truth.

I had come out to my parents the year before. When I told Dad that I was contemplating early resignation, he counseled me to stay in the Navy, even though he knew my sexual orientation. "You'll make captain, Beth, and who knows, perhaps be our first lady admiral." To know me is to know that I wanted to make captain. Since my father was an admiral, I should at least be a captain. My assignment officer told me he was sending me to the Pentagon to a captain's billet, and he expected me to be selected at the next Selection Board meeting. What to do?

My deepest roots from birth were my family and the United States Navy. Yet because I was born a lesbian, I never felt free to be me in the Navy. After twenty-one years of having to hide my sexual orientation, I felt I had little choice but to submit my resignation from the Navy and find other fertile soil in which to plant roots. In order to maintain my integrity, I needed to say. I could no longer live a lie or accept the sword of Damocles hanging over my head. I resigned in September 1980, without making captain.

In the post-Navy years, I began to feel as though I were a free American citizen. I could speak, I could seek, I could cry, and I could be me. But I missed the Navy and those deep roots.

With 1993 came a major political fight over gays in the military, and another unstoppable felt need came from within: to document my work for Navy women's equality and at the same time write about the injustices I experienced as a gay person in the military. I worked on

my book for four years with six other authors, until it was ready for publication. Two contentious issues interfered. First, my father, by now a retired admiral, said, "There are many books in the library, but this should not be one of them. You're a fine thinker. Write about the United Nations or Sino-Soviet relations . . . but definitely not this subject." He knew that publication would out not only me but also him and Mother. The second issue was the use of my name as the primary author. Navy experts had advised me that it was unclear whether military retirees were subject to the "Don't Ask, Don't Tell" (DADT) policy; my pension and benefits might be jeopardized.

After long discussions, my father and I settled our differences. Resolution about the use of my name came in my former minister's office at First Church in San Diego. Rev. Tom Owen-Towle and his wife, Carolyn, were the first Unitarian Universalist ministers I ever met. Tom and I had worked in the Peace Movement together, so I trusted his judgment. After I explained my dilemma about using my real name, Tom looked me straight in the eyes and said, "Beth, take courage." I knew what he was saying. My parents had given me the courage to be myself, whereas Tom's support set me free from fear and paranoia. The more I spoke my truth about my sexual orientation, the freer I became. Speaking my truth became what the military refers to as a force multiplier, an attribute or capability that exponentially increases the impact of an action.

My Navy Too has my name on the cover. In later years, I would learn that retirees are not subject to DADT. At the time, in 1997, publishing a book that once again confronted the entity I called "Big Daddy Navy" and its underlying value system and regulations felt like a huge risk. To question the treatment of Navy women as a feminist was far easier than confronting the military's long-standing policy about gay service members and their "incompatibility with the armed services" as a lesbian. Nonetheless, as my mother would often say, "To live without risk is not to live at all."

In the larger sense, can one speak up only for women and not for other less fortunate groups? No!

In 1995, I joined the Rogue Valley Unitarian Universalist Fellowship (RVUUF) in Ashland, Oregon. Through the years, our congregation has gradually become strongly committed to working for LGBT justice, including becoming a Welcoming Congregation. In the past decade, our community has gained many LGBT members, which feels right to me, as RVUUF's "lesbian elder."

I've felt fully supported by my fellow congregants in my work to repeal DADT. Along with partners, friends, and family members, they have been force multipliers, strengthening my courage to speak candidly at both local and national levels.

Being a member of a Unitarian Universalist congregation has deepened by own belief system, a sort of spirituality that Dr. Timothy Conway calls "engaged spirituality." In the April 2003 issue of *The Sun*, Conway writes of two kinds of spirituality: mystical and engaged. He defines engaged spirituality as "working for the public good or collective welfare, out of a deep sense of solidarity of all sentient beings." I would describe myself as practicing engaged spirituality with a strong leaning toward engaged patriotism.

Spirituality, like patriotism, is not something that you inherit or catch, like the flu. It's something you grow. My participation as a member of RVUUF and as an engaged patriot, coupled with encouragement from many Unitarian Universalists locally and nationally, has grown my spirituality quotient and lifted my spirits. The angst and disappointment of resigning early from the Navy have been superseded by the love and warmth of being among others who understand LGBT matters and who proactively take strategic social action.

In the past five years, I have taken my faith, my engaged spirituality, and my patriotism into the wider world by speaking out and writing about repeal of DADT at both the local and national levels. Some days I'm a broken record and a one-issue activist; however, I've also written about why we must not elect Sarah Palin as vice president and why the Iraq War has similarities to Vietnam.

I learned many years ago that the pen can be as powerful as the sword, although the writer must be prepared to receive wounds just as soldiers and sailors do on the battlefield and in enemy waters. Indeed, one endures a form of combat in responding to the attacks on justice, freedom, and equality across the country's radio waves, in the halls of Congress, or in cyberspace.

Occasionally, bitter and ugly attacks against me appear on the Internet, and I think of my Unitarian Universalist and LGB veteran friends, who embolden me to stand up and be counted. I'm not alone anymore. I also remember my learning from seventies feminism: The turtle never gets ahead without sticking her neck out.

Political cries to repeal DADT were heard early in 2010. Senior military officers, such as the commandant of the Marine Corps, went public against repeal. I felt the need to fight back, defending those 65,000 or more LGB service members who serve in silence and in fear of losing their careers. When Military.com's headline, "Lesbian Vet Decries Living a Lie" (about my own life), came across my computer monitor, I flinched and had to remember Tom Owen-Towle's supportive call to arms, "Take courage."

In spring 2010, as congressional votes for and against repeal were about to be counted, I came up with the idea of sending letters to key officials at the Pentagon, Capitol Hill, and the White House from LGB military veterans on the Military Outreach Committee. This collection of personal stories, titled *We Are Family Too* and written by thirty-seven LGB vets from all services, is an eloquent, powerful statement of why DADT must be repealed. The Committee made certain that *We Are Family Too* landed on the desks of many influential political and military leaders. Our voices were heard; the House voted to repeal DADT.

The struggles of other denominations to respond to LGBT issues look very different from those of Unitarian Universalism and the more liberal religions. In the spring of 2010, I participated in the annual meeting of the Forum of Military Chaplaincy, a group of military chaplains, academics, and line officers who were initiating actions in support of repealing DADT. After the gathering, I asked a retired Air Force senior chaplain, "How many military chaplains are to the right or not moderate?" His answer appalled me: "At least 60 to 70 percent."

These chaplains serve a broad slice of military Americans whose religious faiths are definitely not 60- to 70-percent to the right. Evangelical chaplains have flooded our military in recent decades, with only a minority chaplain presence from the more moderate to liberal clergy. All three chiefs of chaplains were against repeal of DADT, for example. They and many other chaplains from conservative faiths believe gay identity is incompatible with church teachings and, therefore, with military service. We have a long way to go to return to a Chaplain Corps that is able to serve all service people. In 2011, the total number of Unitarian Universalist chaplains, both active duty and reserves, within the Chaplain Corps of about 2,900 officers, is 13.

The clash between many military chaplains' personal beliefs and national policy has been heightened by the historic repeal of Don't Ask, Don't Tell. I remember the day the Senate voted, Saturday, December 18, 2010. I awoke at 5:45 a.m. with great anticipation. Several friends and I watched the proceedings as my senator, Democrat Ron Wyden, spoke from the Senate floor: "I don't care who you love. . . . If you love your country enough to risk your life, you shouldn't have to hide who you are." When the final vote came, repeal passed 65 to 31, with 8 Republicans joining the Democratic majority. Champagne glasses in hand, tears streaming, my friends and I shared a long hug. Our time had come!

I am proud of Americans, gay and straight, who worked to bring equality and justice to the lives of lesbian, gay, and bisexual military members. These service members no longer will be required to serve in silence. At last, I am able to close the chapter of fifty years of my life and truly feel that it's my Navy too!

In the 1980s, I taught college-level political theory and rediscovered Plato's Allegory of the Cave, which I'd first pondered in my own sophomore philosophy class. The essence of Plato's allegory: All humans have filters that can give us false perceptions of the real world, and, although the prisoners in his cave, as described in *The Republic*, truly believe they are seeing real objects, the figures they see are in fact distorted. When a prisoner escapes into the light of day and sees real forms, he "can perceive the true form of reality rather than the mere shadows seen by the prisoners."

To belong to a liberal religious faith is to participate in pulling off those tainted filters about the LGBT community.

The Unitarian Universalist Association, its affiliates, and congregations, including my own, work tirelessly and have succeeded in large measure toward clearing up misperceptions about LGBT persons, encouraging all to walk out of the cave.

My own filters regarding homosexuality have changed dramatically over the years. It wasn't until I stepped out of the cave, the military's subculture around homosexuality, that I became more comfortable accepting myself as different from the majority of my culture. Over the past forty years, I've revealed my sexual orientation to many straight friends and family members. What I know from these discussions is that Americans are beginning to take off their heterosexist filters and recognize that their friends and family members who happen to have been born nonheterosexual are really okay and just like themselves in every other way.

After reading *My Navy Too*, my dad said to me, "You had no choice in the matter, did you?" My decisions not to marry and not to remain on active duty centered around my sexual orientation. My deep Navy roots were torn asunder. But today other roots hold me close, especially those I've grown as a Unitarian Universalist practicing engaged spirituality.

Rev. Tom Owen-Towle's wisdom and encouragement, love from family and friends, self-esteem nurtured by my parents, love and support from my fellow Unitarian Universalists, and my longtime companion and Wellesley classmate of over thirty years have all helped to set me free and lead me to an important discovery. As Wayne Arnason writes in a reading from the Unitarian Universalist hymnbook, "Take courage friends. The way is often hard, the path is never clear, and the stakes are very high. Take courage. For deep down, there is another truth, you are not alone."

—◆—

BETH F. COYE *earned a BA in political science from Welles-
ley College, an MA in international relations from American
University, and a Certificate in Naval Warfare from the Naval
War College, Newport, Rhode Island. She has taught at several
colleges and universities, including the Naval War College;
Mesa College, San Diego; San Diego State College; and the
University of San Diego. Her academic fields include American government, international relations, women's studies, and
human resource management. In twenty-one years as a U.S.
Navy line officer, Commander Coye served three tours in Intelligence, and she was one of the Navy's first female commanding
officers. She has published articles in the* Naval War College
Review *and the Naval Institute's Proceedings. Since her Navy
retirement, she has been an active leader in the Rogue Valley
Unitarian Universalist Church, where she is past president and
currently chair of the Council of Ministries. She is the editor of
both* My Navy Too, *which addresses issues related to minorities in the military, and* We Are Family Too, *a collection of
letters written by gay service members. She currently serves on
the Forum on the Military Chaplaincy and has been featured
in Military.com.*

For We Are Strong

Kate Griffin

I was born in 1940 in Stanly County, North Carolina. Both sets of grandparents were farmers. In that time and place, there were clear rules about what was right and what was wrong and how people had to act, depending on their gender. Jim Crow laws and all the harsh, cruel discrimination based on color permeated our mutual web of existence. In addition, of course, power based on wealth imposed its control on society just as it does today.

One of my early memories of childhood was my cousin Mary teaching me a song in her garage. For some reason, I insisted on singing, "Yes, Jesus loves me, for he is weak and we are strong!"

When I was five years old, I announced that I was going to be like my aunt Carrie and never get married. Carrie was unique among my sixteen aunts and uncles: The rest all got married and liked it so much that several tried it two and three times.

In a studio photograph on the back of which my mother wrote that I was three years old, I am dressed in a sundress and have blond hair in Shirley Temple curls. My eyes are burning with anger, and I have one hand on my knee in the classic studio pose of the day, with one leg folded under me. My left hand is clutching my knee tightly, little nails pushing into the flesh. My free foot is kicking. When I was older and tired of answering the question, "When did you come out?" I chose this photo as proof that it took place in a photography studio when I was three.

My guess is that the term *coming out* was coined in the late 1970s or in the 1980s, because I was not living in the

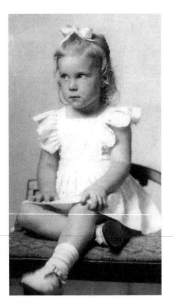

United States when it happened. I was already in my fifties when I was first asked about coming out. I thought it was a strange question, one that it has taken me years to understand.

I like to think that I knew and accepted that I was different. My childhood was harsh and difficult. I suffered abuse of many kinds, but I also believed that I had a titanium core that would preserve me. I was brought up in a very rigid household in what I have always thought of as a puritanical society. But many adults did not act the way I was taught that our Puritan ancestors acted. There were no Puritan stocks for the adult males I grew up around, and perhaps I learned from them the thrill of breaking rigid rules and having big secrets. At age seven, I began secretly smoking and even taught my four-year-old brother how! I will let the therapists among my readers deal with why breaking the rules was so exciting at my age. Over the years, several have helped me deal with why it was also sometimes extremely sad and depressing.

Maybe I was already rebelling against the way things were because the way things were did not empower me. Women were second-class citizens everywhere I looked— except Aunt Carrie. Not only did she not have children but she drove a clean, new car and lived in an apartment in the city because she was a secretary. She did not work in a cotton mill or the fields; she dressed up and went to an air-conditioned office where she used a typewriter and worked with men who had clean fingernails!

Hunting season was a particular favorite of mine because it might mean squirrel or rabbit stew for dinner. The men took the rifles and a shotgun, bought new shells, gathered in groups, and went off into the woods. Whatever the men killed, they "cleaned," which usually meant skinning it, but the women cooked it. After meals, men squatted in the yard, smoking cigarettes and laughing. Women washed dishes in the kitchen. I remember with joy one Thanksgiving when I begged so much that I got to go hunting with the men! The funny thing is I have no memory of whether or not they bagged anything. The thrill was in stepping into a role that was normally out of bounds simply because "girls don't do that."

The division of duties by gender was relaxed when men joined—no, when they "helped"—the women. Please consider the subtle difference. In the summer, many hot, dusty days meant gardening in some form. When the green beans in Grandpa Griffin's garden were ready, whoever was available would pick them in the hot afternoon sun. After work and an early supper, a happier ritual would begin. Aunts and uncles would show up. We would gather outside in the backyard and sit in straight wooden chairs pulled into a circle. We'd all get a section of the newspaper for our lap, fill it with beans, and begin to string them, break them, and throw them into a pot. Lots of talk would go on, mostly about what had happened during the day. It could be a harsh time for a kid because the adult men were without mercy. I'd try my best to keep quiet rather than say anything that would make an uncle notice me and say, "What's that, little Lacy Drawers?"

Those nights in family, those stories often repeated, and those hours of working together gave me something that made me strong, because I knew where I belonged. I had roots and rituals, even the teasing, and an acceptance that gave me strength to overcome the pain and suffering that those same people caused me. It is all in my heart still.

In the country, the two largest social events were the local high school basketball games on Friday nights, where all denominations met, and church on Sunday mornings, which separated us all. Most of what I learned in church left me feeling bad about myself. Most of what I did on the basketball court made me feel pretty good. I liked the applause and trophies!

As I entered later adolescence, I became melancholic. I guess that is a requirement of that age. In those days, boys asked girls on dates. Girls sat and waited to be invited somewhere, anywhere. The boys I was attracted to did not ask me out, and the boys who did were boring. I found it much more fun to be with girls, but then again, one was expected to date, so I did. There was really no other way to be, back there in my world. We did not read Sappho down on the farm.

In 1958, I attended a small college in the Appalachian Mountains, and there I found hints of other ways to be. I began to find it exciting to defy my Presbyterian junior college rules. Sometimes, during Sunday afternoon study lockdown, we would smoke a cigar, driving the dorm mother crazy while she looked for the man who had snuck in. I dated boys—and began to learn there were girls who were having some kind of closer relationship with each other than I had ever heard of or even read about. In fact, my roommate was being "comforted" by a sophomore. Mind you, she needed, she deserved, even more tenderness in her life than I did because her life had been very,

very hard. Still, I was fascinated by this comforting. Since no sophomore seemed interested in becoming close to me and I was not one to be put into a box, I decided to take the lead! My best friend, a freshman, and I began to experiment with kissing. Very wild!

Even so, the college was as controlling as home had been. Everyone had to go to church on Sunday night, and girls had to wait for the dean of women to give permission for them to wear pants, even when it was snowing! Girls were required to be in the dorm or the library on weeknights, and lights went out when the dorm mother came by and knocked on the door. So, although kissing a girl was hardly a totally sexual experiment, I now find it ironic that my first steps of acting on my true sexual orientation were liberated by the very strictness of the Presbyterian school that had tried to control me too much. Oh, I continued to date a football player and was even in the Valentine Court, wearing a frilly gown, so the outside did not change. Nevertheless, I was forever changed inside.

My other life-altering experience in college was studying the Bible as a document rather than as the word of God. I could not put what I had learned as a child into the context of what I was now beginning to learn. After all, the instructor was a Presbyterian minister, and I had been taught to respect and believe what ministers said. His words at first created total disbelief in my heart, but they were logical, so my mind wrapped around this new way of looking at the only guidebook everyone I had grown up with expounded on as the one way, the truth. I loved learning that it was perhaps someone's version of a truth, but that was as far as reason allowed me to go. I was now becoming someone entirely different, not only from who I had been but, seemingly, from everyone I had known in the first eighteen years of my life.

It's demoralizing to admit that I was seduced by a freshman girl the next year, when I was a sophomore. That was the first passionate and loving encounter of my life, and everything about it was secret and hidden. We were never caught making love (thank goodness there were no video cameras and cell phones then), but it was probably not a secret to many people.

That began my pattern of secret affairs with women. I was hardly a shy, quiet person, but I learned early on to live another life quietly as I navigated society's restrictions. Later, I would learn that generations before me—and unfortunately some after me—had also practiced "Don't Ask, Don't Tell."

College over, I easily found a "Don't Ask, Don't Tell" career: I became a high school teacher. I taught English in a senior high school of 2,300 in Baltimore County, Maryland. There were no gay faculty members or students. After all, from 1962 to 1967, awareness of gay identity had not yet reached Baltimore County. So, by day I was an English teacher—no need to say "straight" because we all were—and in my time off, I was secretly queer. This double life was fun and exciting. Most of the time. It was also sometimes extremely sad and depressing to be gay, because there was no such thing. My gayness did not exist because it did not have a name. Ellen DeGeneres did not live next door, much less have a TV show. What made me me was not reflected anywhere, much less accepted. Needless to say, I did not go to church. No reason to add to my invisibility: "Come in, child of God, but leave your sexual orientation outside the door, please."

In 1965, *The Baltimore Sun* was to help change it all. Not immediately, but eventually. Reading the Sunday paper was always a joy, but reading every damn article was also an obligation. I even read the religion pages. I kept noticing stuff happening at the "Unitarian" Church. One Sunday, I decided to go.

Up to that day, I had never been in anything other than our small country Protestant churches or the large decorated, stately Catholic churches of Baltimore to attend first communions and other rites. Wow, this First Unitarian Church of Baltimore was big! It was grand and beautiful, but there was no bloody Christ hanging on a cross. I had assumed that a big impressive church would have the Virgin along with a guy hanging on a cross to keep you sad. Not so.

That day, the minister, whose name I have unfortunately forgotten, talked about the afterlife. He said something that I had never heard from a preacher, something like this: "I have no idea what will really happen when I die, but I hope that my body will serve to nourish the roots of an oak tree and that my life will continue in that way. After all, I've admired some oak trees more than a lot of people I have known!" Oh, my God! No preacher I had ever heard had admitted that he was uncertain about anything! No heaven and hell to separate good from bad?

I started attending, but not regularly, because that habit had been broken. There were many things to do on a Sunday in Baltimore, and I was born to do them all.

However, I had glimpsed another world. Unfortunately, I was not yet ready to dive into it, although my soul now knew something different. When I had stopped going to church in my adolescence, I believed there was no reason to walk through church doors again. The preacher had made us feel so small that we could have easily crawled out under the door. However, here was a place of laughter, not tears; a place of life, not death; a place where real love was possible, not a pious, condescending, phony love based on what I could be molded into but love for who I already was!

I left Baltimore. After teaching for nine years in Alachua, Florida, a cross was burned on my lawn in 1969, not because I was queer but because, with my liberal views and black friends, I didn't fit in. The funny thing was that I knew the boys who did it. They were caught because they came back to make sure the fire did not spread to my little frame house. But when I told the sheriff that it was a joke, he said, "We don't take it as a joke here." Indeed, because of the cross burning, I was perceived as a liability to the school system. The principal told me that, although I was chair of the English Department and, in his words, "one of the best teachers I've ever had," I just did not "fit in." Parents were going to protest at the county school board if I wanted to return the following year to teach. I vowed to leave the country.

I passed the Foreign Service entrance exam in the summer of 1971, and became a Foreign Service Information Officer. As a diplomat, I was really, really in "Don't Ask, Don't Tell" territory big time; gay people were viewed as dangerous liabilities by my employer, the U.S. Information Agency. After all, our "lifestyle" left us open to blackmail. We were security risks of the worst kind. I served in Ethiopia and Cameroon. I was successful and received rapid promotions to higher grades. I even shook the hand of the Rastafarians' god, Haile Selassie, the emperor of Ethiopia, whose palace was through the eucalyptus grove behind my apartment and whose lions I could hear roar in the early morning.

For many reasons, I refused a promotion to a post in Cape Town, South Africa, and quit the Foreign Service in 1975. The main reason was to follow a woman to France. Finally, I dared to become the same person by day as by night. I lived with Françoise and her two children for twelve years. Paris even boasted a small group of Unitarians (mostly ex-pat Americans), and I attended services a few times. But it was more meaningful for me to be accepted into Françoise's family and by French friends. I was no longer obliged to lead a double life. The French are tolerant of many things, except fools.

When I returned to the United States in 1989, I discovered that much had happened during my seventeen years abroad. Even though I had returned stateside to visit almost every year, I was unaware of the depth of these changes.

I returned to teaching by taking a position as an English instructor at Tuskegee University in Alabama. I was politically and socially very comfortable in that historically black institution. In addition, I immediately joined the Unitarian Universalist Fellowship of Auburn.

It was everything I had dreamed of in a spiritual home, even though I was not ready to use that language yet. I was a secular humanist and proud of it in the midst of all my conservative Christian friends. The small congregation was made up of couples, including one lesbian couple; singles, including a few of us single queers; and lots of children. Even though our sanctuary had been built by freed slaves and had served a black congregation, from whom we purchased it, we were a group of white folk. However, I lived in an integrated apartment complex and worked with an all-black student body and an overwhelmingly black faculty at Tuskegee. From those vantage points, I actually was impressed with the progress the South had made.

Many people laughed when they learned that I had come to Alabama from France. But I was home in so many ways. The South was a place that I had had to leave in order to become authentic, but it was my culture, and I loved those hot muggy days. I had left the church, but now I was back because I had found one that thought laughter in church was alright. This church encouraged people to think. There was no dogma. And I had never forgotten that Unitarian minister from First Baltimore in the 1960s. Finally, there was no one standing in front of me saying, "This is the only way to live, to love, to be."

I became a Unitarian Universalist evangelist. I was successful, and a few years later, I moved to Boston to work for the Unitarian Universalist Women's Federation (UUWF). In that wonderful job, part of my role was to be who I was! I was suddenly queer—a word I had never used to describe myself before—because this was Boston. Now, I was not only out but encouraged to bring other nonheterosexual women into the UUWF!

Boston, home of group meetings such as the Coming out Group, the Wives of Bisexual Husbands, The Lesbian Avengers. . . . Ah, Boston: a very tolerant place? Sure! No, but that is weak: a very accepting place. A place where differences are as common as a Republican governor every year and an overwhelmingly Democratic House and Senate. The home of Barney Frank!

I was half a century old by then. I had been back in the states for five years; I'd become American again. I was intrigued by my new home, Boston, and excited about my new work which, in my mind, made me a Unitarian Universalist missionary of sorts. I was reaching out to create new women's groups in Unitarian Universalist churches all over the United States and Canada, or to revive the groups where only older women attended. And I had such resources at my fingertips because I worked at the Unitarian Universalist Association headquarters. Just two blocks away was the very large Arlington Street Church, which had a lesbian minister, Rev. Kim K. Crawford Harvie. She was the first lesbian minister I had heard deliver a sermon. Seeing her mount that elevated chancel surrounded by those Tiffany windows and knowing the history stored in the walls of that place was an awesome experience.

I wanted to bring this amazing lesbian minister a bit of my history and perhaps get some guidance in my new work. So I went to a counseling session with Kim. When I told her my story of leaving France and Françoise, Sophie, and Hervé, she replied, "Oh, what a loss for you. How sad to give up your entire family." What? I was stunned. Pretty much everyone had been delighted to see me back in the states; few really had any idea how difficult it was to leave my family. Some had asked me if I missed France. No one, except my brother and sister and a few close friends, had asked my feelings about leaving a woman I had loved for seventeen years and the family of four we had created. I had opted to deny my pain. It seemed inappropriate to miss my French family when I was so happy to be back home. As a minister, Kim invited me not only to admit my loss but to mourn it. Finally, I could grieve. I had lost so much; I still remember the pain I was allowed to release in that moment. I had taken another step in that strange act of coming out.

I was home, finally. I was queer and I did not need forgiveness from the church for that. No one prayed for me because of that. As a gay/queer Unitarian Universalist, I was not only accepted, I was welcomed.

Today I live in Wilmington, North Carolina, on the Cape Fear River. Tell me that doesn't sound like an exciting place to be! It really is. The Unitarian Universalist Fellowship of Wilmington started forty years ago with fourteen people, has grown to 250 members, and is steadily attracting new ones. Now, here is the irony I want to share: Several Sundays ago, one of our thirteen-year-olds asked me if I would be her honorary grandmother. I accepted, of course. To honor this relationship, we went to lunch after the service.

That day, Rev. Cheryl M. Walker's sermon was about how we could attempt to relieve the hatred in a world where

too many very young boys had committed suicide because they were perceived as gay. She told of her rejection from the religious community she grew up in, especially from the pastor, because of her lesbianism. As we drove to lunch, my grandchild said, "I didn't know that Rev. Cheryl was gay." She spoke in the same intonation in which she would have said, "I didn't know that you had a white car." Normal tone. Normal inflection.

"Oh, you didn't?" I said, with a bit of surprise, because Cheryl has always been out.

"You do know that I am gay, don't you?" I continued.

"No," was her reply, again in a normal tone.

Knowing that something in young people, even here in my beloved Southland, has shifted toward acceptance brings me such gratitude and joy. I am just another human being. I do not have to hide in a box of another name. That moment will always be in my heart.

Did you know the ancient Egyptians removed all organs when they mummified a body—except the heart? They left that for use in the afterlife. They thought that it was the center of intelligence and emotion.

Unitarian Universalists take pride in being rational, intellectual. We sometimes place the brain at the center of our being, but I agree with the Egyptians. The center of our being is the heart.

‹o›

KATE GRIFFIN *was the only girl from her high school class and the first in her extended family to attend college. She taught high school English in Baltimore County. Around 1964, she discovered the downtown Baltimore's Unitarian Church and became a Unitarian Universalist. She describes herself as "a mix of intellectual and service station mechanic." After earning a master of liberal arts degree at Johns Hopkins University,* *she became the English Department chair in Alachua, Florida. After a cross was burned on her lawn in the midst of school desegregation, she left the United States and became a Foreign Service information officer, working in Ethiopia and Cameroon. She fell in love and lived with a French woman for twelve years, and was director of the Berlitz School of Languages in Paris. In 1989, she returned to the United States and taught English at Tuskegee University. She joyfully discovered the Auburn (Alabama) Unitarian Universalist Fellowship. In 1994, she became director of Communication and Membership for the Unitarian Universalist Women's Federation, in Boston. The UUWF board eliminated all staff positions in November 1996, and Griffin stopped participating in Unitarian Universalism. She became an investment associate at UBSPaineWebber, but eventually returned to the South and to Unitarian Universalism, becoming a member of the Fellowship of Wilmington, North Carolina, in 2004. She has co-led the Welcoming Congregation seminar and taught religious education.*

CROSSING THE RUBICON

KATHLEEN ROBBINS

Football letterman, Eagle Scout, Air Force Academy graduate, husband to a wonderful woman, Vietnam veteran, proud parent: How many ways could I run away from something that had been a huge part of my life since I was three or four years old—something that I knew was wrong, shameful, and impossible? Yet a deep knowledge drew me closer and closer, the more I denied the reality and sought to distance myself. I was a woman.

This story starts with the military. I reported to the Air Force Academy at the end of June 1964, three weeks after graduating from high school. The Gulf of Tonkin Resolution that authorized U.S. military assistance in Vietnam passed Congress in August 1964. I spent four years at the Academy "drinking the Kool-Aid," believing what I was told. We were in Vietnam for "nation building and protecting the people against Communism."

After graduation from the Air Force Academy, I went to

navigator training, married my college sweetheart in December 1968, and was flying C-130 cargo airplanes in Vietnam by September 1969. I was assigned to a squadron flying out of the Philippines, "commuting to war," spending fifteen days in Vietnam at a time. That way, we didn't count against the number of military personnel Congress had authorized to be there. We did everything from carrying sick and wounded to dropping 15,000-pound bombs called "daisy cutters," the largest conventional weapons in the U.S. inventory.

In March 1970, Prince Sihanouk was overthrown in a U.S.-sponsored coup d'état and General Lon Nol was installed. The United States began flying military supplies into Cambodia. On my first flight in, I knew, despite U.S. denials, that a major bombing campaign was going on: The rice fields looked like the surface of the moon, filled with craters. At the same time, a massive buildup was happening in the "parrot's beak," the area along the border between Vietnam and Cambodia. On the evening of April 30, 1970, I found myself in the air over Cambodia, loaded with a daisy cutter. We dropped the bomb right across the border at dawn to make a helicopter landing zone. Whether by design or by accident, our bomb set off a secondary explosion that was larger than the original; we had hit an underground ammunition dump. For that flight, I was awarded the Distinguished Flying Cross. In hindsight, I have to live with the reality that my actions in some way may have contributed to the dictator Pol Pot seizing power in Cambodia, resulting in the deaths of millions of Cambodians.

My son was born in May 1971, and I finished my two years flying between the Philippines and Vietnam, returning stateside in the fall of 1971. The huge antiwar demonstrations made me angry. I had done my duty; why didn't people understand that? Why were they angry at me? I remained in the Air Force until the summer of 1975, teaching navigation and completing an MBA. Saigon fell to the North Vietnamese in April 1975. I resigned in July 1975 and thought I was moving on.

Despite my stereotypically male behavior and loving Julie very much, my gender identity issues plagued our marriage. Right before getting out of the Air Force, I finally agreed to see a therapist. I lived in fear that the military would find out about my "problem," as she called it. I went to a civilian therapist and paid out of pocket so it wouldn't show up on my military record. The therapist recommended "aversion therapy." Rather than give me shock treatment or something like that, he designed an approach that would create emotional pain for Julie. I was to cross-dress in front of her. Sure enough, the evident pain it caused her

helped reduce my desire to transition.

As harsh as it was, the effectiveness of the therapist's approach lasted for only six months. I very reluctantly accepted the reality that my "feelings" were not going to go away, and I began to transition from male to female in 1980. The universe, however, had other plans. Two months into my hormone therapy, my carefully orchestrated world came to a crashing halt: Julie was diagnosed with a brain tumor. Our son Tim was nine at the time, and I quickly put aside any considerations of moving forward with the transition to take care of them.

I had never really had to deal up close and personal with the prospect of death. As I was growing up, my immediate family was healthy. Even in two years of flying in Vietnam, no one close to me was hurt, let alone killed. My religious education offered little help. I had grown up in the Presbyterian Church. Julie and I were members of a Methodist church when her tumor appeared, but religion was more a social thing, not central to my life. I had tried to live by the golden rule but had never really had my faith tested in a meaningful way. Now I found myself in a situation with few, if any, coping strategies and a secret identity I felt I couldn't share with my closest friends, and my best friend—my wife—was dying.

We were told the tumor was inoperable and that she probably had a year to live. Radiation was the only recommended treatment, and its effectiveness would be short-lived at best. We were told in a very kind way, but the message was clear: Go home and prepare to die. I came to understand the term *foxhole Christian* in ways I had never experienced in Vietnam. I went through all the classic stages of grief. As Julie went through the diagnostic labyrinth, I asked the typical questions: Why her? Why me? Why now? I prayed to God (the old man on the throne from Sunday school) to spare her. I tried to make a bargain. If only he would spare Julie, I would never again consider transitioning. I would be good, whatever that meant!

Over the summer of 1980, while Julie endured a massive and disabling course of radiation, I researched alternative treatments. Long before the Internet was available, I had to research the old-fashioned way, with phone calls and letters. It was painfully slow, but it gave me something to do. A doctor in the Bahamas had been featured on *60 Minutes* soon after Julie's diagnosis. He didn't promise a cure, but his technique offered a modicum of hope, something we were desperate to find. Besides, what did we have to lose? We asked Julie's neurosurgeon about any downsides or danger. The only response he could come up with was, "You might gain weight, and insurance probably wouldn't cover it." Fortunately, we could afford to pay for the treatment.

During the next seven years, Julie seemed to get better. We moved to Dallas, where we owned a company, and when it failed, I took a job with Wang Computers. I also returned to therapy to try again to deal with my gender-identity issues.

Married almost twenty years, Julie and I decided to separate in 1987. I had just turned forty, and her brain tumor seemed to be gone, according to the latest CT scan. We still loved each other, but she said, "I'm not a lesbian," so being in a relationship with me as a woman was not an option for her. My acceptance of my true gender had begun to feel comfortable; I was anxious to move on with my life. It was now or never. Julie seemed healthy, Tim was a sophomore in high school, and I wasn't getting any younger.

Within six weeks of our separation, Julie collapsed at a church picnic; the tumor was back. Once again, I felt I had to choose between being myself and taking care of her. This time, I chose to continue with my transition, caring for Julie while living separately. The decision to continue transitioning is one I struggle with to this day. I had made a commitment to her "in sickness and in health." Yet I couldn't just forget who I was. Only after I accepted that there wasn't a right answer did I feel free to move forward.

When I told my therapist of the return of Julie's tumor, he responded by saying that I had caused it. I left his office crying. On the drive back to work, I was a total wreck. I found myself looking for a bridge abutment to ram my car into. It was the closest I've ever come to suicide, but even as I despaired, I remembered Tim and that my death would mean he had lost both parents. He didn't deserve that. The next day, I returned to the therapist and told him what had almost happened and what I thought of his therapeutic methods. I never saw him again.

I found a different therapist and began to get deeply

involved in a new Methodist church. (Julie "got" our former church when we separated). Much to my surprise, this new church was a stop on a twentieth-century version of the Underground Railroad. The ministers and several members were helping refugees from the war in El Salvador move north to Canada where, unlike in the United States, they would be granted asylum.

Although I liked, trusted, and believed the ministers, I had trouble accepting what they were saying about U.S. actions they had observed in El Salvador, I still believed that we—the United States—were the good guys and gals and wouldn't do what the ministers were saying. So, as with most things in my life, the more I studied, the more I knew I didn't know. The only way to resolve this dilemma was to see for myself.

Julie passed away in February 1989, and Tim graduated from high school that May. I continued to prepare to transition—and at the same time wanted to run away from even the thought of it. I headed to Florida to tell my sister about my plans to transition on a weekend in August that coincided with my twenty-fifth high school reunion.

I went to the reunion and reconnected with one of my classmates, Nicole, who had recently divorced. Before the evening was over, I told her about my plans to transition from male to female. Rather than being repelled or appalled, she was accepting; I was so surprised! At the same time, the urge to change went away, as it had several times in the past. I prayed it would be permanent this time.

We began an intense long-distance relationship. Nicole lived in Florida and I in Texas, so we traveled back and forth as well as talking and emailing daily. Everything seemed so good and normal, yet the "feelings" returned. In the spring of 1990, Nicole and I took a cruise together. Toward the end, I told her I had begun taking hormones. Suddenly, all she wanted to be was friends. When we parted, I knew it was more important to be true to myself than to be in the relationship. Still, loneliness has been the most difficult part of my journey.

In the fall of 1990, I decided to visit El Salvador. Several weeks before I left, I told Tim about my impending gender change. It was the hardest thing I've ever had to do. Tears came to his eyes. He had lost his mom only a year before, and now I was throwing this at him! I explained as well as I could why I felt I had to make the journey from male to female. I quit my job at Wang, just as the company began to fail.

With the hormone treatments that I had begun in the United States, I would come back from El Salvador as "Kathleen." It dawned on me that I needed legal approval for my name and gender change to get a new job when I returned, unless I wanted to out myself on my first day. So right before leaving the United States, I filed the necessary paperwork with the court in Dallas. I had crossed the Rubicon with no practical way back; it was a very scary feeling, much scarier than being shot at in Vietnam. There, I would only die, not be continually humiliated.

As part of the preparation for the trip, the minister asked everyone in the group that was going to watch a video about an American medical doctor who had gone to El Salvador in 1982 and worked with noncombatants trapped in the war zone. The video, *Witness to War,* was based on a book by Dr. Charlie Clements. Imagine my surprise when one of the first images on the screen was of cadets marching at the U.S. Air Force Academy. I wondered what had taken him from the skies of Vietnam to the jungle in El Salvador.

In El Salvador, I learned about war from the ground level and began to confront the reality of geopolitics, how it affected human life, and my responsibilities as a human being.

On our first day there, my group went to the University of Central America to meet with a Jesuit priest who replaced one of the six murdered by members of the U.S.-trained Salvadoran army. He related that one of the killers had told of coming to the locked gate, beginning to "blow it down," when a priest came out and calmly unlocked it, saying, "I know why you have come." Six priests, plus the housekeeper and her daughter, were taken into the garden, forced to kneel, and shot. I've always wondered about my reaction to a situation like that. All I can think of is fight or flight, never calm resignation—amazing!

The following day there was a huge demonstration in the capital city, San Salvador, marking the tenth anniversary of the murder of Salvadoran archbishop Oscar Romero. The rest of our group had participated in peace demonstrations before, but this was my first. The armed soldiers along the route, the military helicopters flying overhead, and the photographers taking pictures of the crowd made it a surreal experience.

That night, fighting erupted between the Salvadoran Army and the Frente Farabundo Martí para la Liberación Nacional (FMLN). Our Methodist church group spent the night sleeping on the floor. I had experienced firefights outside my door in Vietnam, but at least there we had Korean marines, U.S. Army soldiers, or as a last resort, U.S.A.F. Air Policemen to protect us. Here we were on our own, just as Salvadoran civilians had been for years.

The next morning, we were off to San Antonio Los Rancho, a small community that the U.S. Embassy said was held by FMLN rebels. The Embassy warned us not to go because they could not help if we encountered trouble along the way. We really didn't know how much danger we were putting ourselves in. It is very lonely when you come to a road blocked by teenagers holding automatic weapons, and you are totally unprotected. We had to navigate four of these roadblocks.

The villagers of San Antonio Los Rancho, having spent nearly ten miserable years in a refugee camp in Honduras, had decided to return and risk dying in their homes rather than continue to endure life as refugees. We spent the night on straw mattresses in a hut as U.S. Army surplus jets, Salvadoran army helicopters, and A-37 bombers flew overhead. The next morning, the mayor gave us a tour of the community. For the first time, I saw the results of an air war up close. We saw the remains of the bombed-out school, church, and clinic. We saw the community garden, one of the elements that made this a "communist haven," according to the U.S. Embassy. Every able-bodied person was required to give a day of labor per week to the community vegetable plot, with the produce going to those who could not work themselves—the old, the sick, and the physically disabled. Nothing in the two years I had spent in Vietnam at 20,000 feet compared to being on the ground in a war zone.

The next day, we returned to San Salvador and flew back to Dallas. Upon my return, I learned that the request for my name and gender change had been approved. While still processing the courage and the lies I had encountered in El Salvador, I was stepping off on my own journey into the unknown. The memory of the courage of the people in San Antonio served as a vivid reminder throughout the fear and doubt of my transition. I realized that, like them, I must be willing to take life-changing risks and be true to myself to live with integrity. My challenge has been, and continues to be, discerning my truth and accepting that my truth might hurt others.

Upon returning, I had to find a job. I wasn't particularly worried about how people felt in the government offices as I changed my name and gender paperwork, but I was really worried about changing the lease on my apartment and job hunting. After all, this was Dallas, Texas, a place not particularly known for liberalism.

I was so worried about job hunting that I decided to start in Houston. At least if I were laughed out of an office there, word wouldn't get around Dallas quickly. I changed only my name on my resume, and I omitted my time in Vietnam. A week or so after returning from El Salvador, I drove to Houston and spent over an hour talking with a headhunter, presenting myself as Kathleen. We really connected; what a relief! She seemed very impressed with my background and experience and was eager to work with me.

When I left the office, I went immediately to the ladies' room. Just as I was coming out of the stall, in walked my interviewer. She looked around the room and, seeing we were alone, said, "Can I ask you a question?" Of course, I already knew her question, but what could I say? I said, "Sure." Then she asked, "Do you ever wear heels? You are striking and should wear them!" Not exactly the question I was expecting! Wow, I had passed! It may sound weird, but my newfound confidence got another boost as I was stopped for speeding on the way back from Houston, and the officer didn't blink at "Kathleen's" new license.

Would I be as lucky when it came to keeping my apartment? I had been a resident since separating from Julie, paid my rent on time, and didn't cause problems, but there was no way to be sure. On the first of the next month, I carried my name change and a check from Kathleen Robbins into the manager's office. He looked at the court paper, handed it back, and thanked me. I was so unprepared for his reaction that I asked, "Do you have any questions?" He answered, "No, this is the nineties!" Wow! Maybe Dallas wouldn't be so bad after all.

Not all tests of my confidence went as well. Immediately after I returned from El Salvador, I made a well-received presentation, in my male identity, on the conditions our group experienced there. When I was asked to do another presentation, I gathered my courage and said I had transitioned to living full-time as my female self. To my amazement, the sponsoring organization didn't seem to have a problem with this information. A strange thing happened with this presentation, though: It seemed to have lost much of its power, I believe because I chose not to relate what I had seen in El Salvador to my experiences in Vietnam, as I had in the first presentation. Hiding my history was a lesson in the pain and loss caused by secrets.

All in all, my transition was remarkably easy. Less than four months after returning from El Salvador and transitioning, I was working in a whole new industry, telecommunications, and had moved to a company-paid apartment in Los Angeles and begun to make new friends there. I was having such a good time in LA that I returned to Texas only every two weeks to pay bills.

One weekend in LA, I came across an invitation to a garden party fundraiser for Physicians for Social Responsibility. Dr. Charlie Clements, president of PSR, was to be the speaker. After reading *Witness to War*, marveling again at Charlie's insight and my lack thereof during the

Vietnam War, I came to the acknowledgments section. Charlie's literary agent's name was Kathy Robbins, the name I had selected for myself the year before. Strange, to say the least.

I went to the party alone, standing head and shoulders above other women in the line to meet Charlie and receive an autographed copy of his book. The moment Charlie saw my name tag, he said, "Did you know—?" I replied with a smile, "Not only do I know about your literary agent but I'm also an Academy grad, and I flew C-130s." Charlie knew two things: Women were not admitted to the Academy when I entered in 1964 (that changed in 1976), and, of course, women didn't fly C-130s in Vietnam.

At the party, Charlie introduced me to one of his best friends from his Vietnam days, Romeo, and Romeo's fiancée Sally. Sally and I hit it off immediately, and we began getting together several times a week. One weekend, Sally and Romeo invited me to attend their church, the First Unitarian Universalist Church of Los Angeles. I had never heard of this religion, but the first time I went, it felt like coming home. I began going to church with Sally and Romeo in Los Angeles and to First Unitarian in Dallas on weekends when I was there. I didn't know anyone in the Dallas church, but the belief in "the inherent worth and dignity of every person" meant that acceptance was never a question. How many people knew or suspected about my transition, I have no idea; I am fortunate that despite being tall, I "pass." I finally got to know people at the church in Dallas while working on a Habitat for Humanity project it sponsored. I was lying side by side under a new set of stairs and became great friends with the woman hammering away beside me. Ann later introduced me to her partner. Together, they introduced me to the world of Unitarian Universalism in Dallas and beyond; they remain wonderful friends.

In 1995, I moved to Illinois to run a small telecommunications company and joined the church in Champaign-Urbana. There, I eventually joined the church board, then the Central Midwest District Board. I also got involved in the local Interweave group (Unitarian Universalists for Gay, Lesbian, Bisexual, and Transgender Concerns) and the national Interweave board. The Church became and remains a big part of my life.

In 1998, I went on an all-women Olivia cruise to Costa Rica with Ann and her partner from Dallas. I was single, so I shared a stateroom with a woman who was taking her third Olivia cruise. She told me her previous roommates had been difficult, and "I was the best one." After four days of getting along great, she suddenly asked if I was transsexual. Rumors had been circulating among her friends on the cruise. I said, "Yes, does it make a difference?"

She was angry; I was devastated and in tears. I skipped dinner and went up on deck. The lights of Costa Rica were in view. I thought about jumping overboard, but I decided it would be a long, cold swim ashore just to escape others' judgments. Later that evening, a brilliant, attractive lesbian I had met sought me out on the bow, and we had a long talk. For the remainder of the cruise, the energy grew between us. We promised to stay in touch after the trip ended, and we did. Was it possible I could find love again?

The relationship between us didn't go far romantically, but it inspired me to try to get involved with lesbian groups when I returned home to Illinois.

I had read about a local lesbian support group and asked one of my church friends who was a member if it was alright for me to come. She said sure but then called me back later and said the group had decided I wasn't welcome. Once again, I was devastated but asked to meet with the group leader to learn their concerns. After a lunch meeting, I was invited to be part of the group; those women are now among my best friends.

I also applied to the doctorate of ministry program that a priest named Matthew Fox had created in Oakland, California. I had no interest in becoming a minister but was attracted by much of Fox's writing, including his *Reinvention of Work*. It also was a doctoral program I could do and still keep my job.

As I proceeded through the program, I asked Charlie Clements to be on my dissertation committee. I discovered that he, too, was a Unitarian Universalist; in fact, later Charlie became president of the Service Committee. I also asked Rev. Jeremy Taylor, a former classmate, ordained Unitarian Universalist minister, and renowned expert on dreamwork, to be on my committee. I graduated in June

2002, and resigned my corporate job in January 2003, to put my beliefs and dreams into action. I went to Haiti to replicate the Grameen Bank phone program, which offers the poor, mainly women, access to modern communications and provides a source of income at the same time. I have been given so many unexpected and undeserved gifts and opportunities in my life, how could I do less?

I completed the village phone program in the summer of 2007, living in Port au Prince for fifteen months.

I am now developing a clean energy program, the Jatropha Pepinye, in rural Haiti. The goal is to create an entirely new value chain with an indigenous perennial plant, *Jatropha curcas*, that will address not only Haiti's energy needs but also rural poverty. Haiti's ecological devastation, combined with destruction of the country's infrastructure by the 2010 earthquake, has made this effort more necessary than ever. The Jatropha Pepinye program goal remains providing support for at least one thousand small growers producing more than one million gallons of biodiesel, providing them with an income four to five times the national average on land that is too harsh for growing food. More important, the Jatropha

Pepinye program provides a model for others to replicate across Haiti.

My journey continues to be amazing. The most remarkable blessing has been the friends and family who have continued to relate with me despite my outward changes. I've made new friends too as I have slowly awakened to the world around me. Doors have opened as I've reached out to connect, and I never know what might be behind the next one. If I hadn't gone to El Salvador, I never would have met Charlie Clements or learned about Unitarian Universalism. Who knows what experiences still await me? I'm still alone, and that is alright. If love comes back into my life, that would be great, but it's not necessary. My life is full. I have my friends, my work, and my faith, all of which embrace me just as I am. What more could a woman ask for?

-◄o►-

KATHLEEN ROBBINS *earned an engineering science degree from the United States Air Force Academy and an MBA while teaching aerial navigation there. She has held positions with Wang Laboratories, Computer Sciences Corporation, and Cellular One of East Central Illinois. To round out her education, she completed a doctorate of ministry program in 2002. Most recently, Robbins led an effort in Haiti to provide access to information communications technology to people living on two dollars or less a day, replicating the hugely successful Grameen Foundation's Village Phone program.*

First It All Falls Apart

Meg Barnhouse

I was fourteen, a student at a girl's prep school where leaded windows opened onto manicured grounds, academic competition was fierce, and the gym teacher was a dour masculine woman rumored to be a lesbian. One of the Seven Sisters colleges was across the street. There was this girl. She decided she loved me and I loved—I loved how much she loved me. It was intense, and a little dangerous. When she would sleep over, my mother let her sleep in my bed. My best friend disapproved, which made me feel independent and rebellious, two feelings I love to this day. This girl would reach out from an otherwise empty classroom, pull me in as I walked by in the hall, and steal kisses until I protested. We never got caught at that; it was the letters she wrote me that caused our downfall. My best friend stole one of them and made copies. For my own good, she said. To snap me out of the spell I was under, she gave copies to all of our classmates.

Her mother mailed one to my parents and to the parents of my lover. My parents didn't do anything that I can recall. Mama probably didn't show it to my dad. I'm guessing she prayed about it the same way she did about the gallon of vodka she found in my sister's closet. Years later, we found out my sister won the vodka at the grocery store where she worked and hadn't wanted to drink it, so she stuck it back in there and forgot about it. So my mom prayed—for what, I'm not sure.

My lover's parents, by contrast, pulled her out of school for a few weeks. She came back, but it was as if someone had ripped out a part of her. I learned years later that they had threatened her with shock treatments and made her go to psychiatrists to cure her "disorder," until she graduated from college. We didn't talk to each other when she came back to school. She was shunned. I wasn't, for some reason. I think my best friend told everyone it wasn't my fault. I'd been seduced, deceived, attacked, really. I couldn't be a lesbian because I wasn't mannish like Miss Tommie, the gym teacher. I started dating my best friend's brother. No one objected to that.

Some years and several boys later, I was engaged to a sweet medical student who played the violin well enough to have had to choose between med school and music school. I didn't feel about him the way I knew I was supposed to feel. I laughed at the songs on the radio that sang of love and desire. Who were they kidding? No one really felt those things. I was at seminary and he was far away, and I liked him, but when we were together, I was mad and miserable. A fellow Presbyterian seminary student was easier to be with. He was handsome and smart, a volleyball-playing philosopher from California. We could talk theology with each other, which was great. I broke up with the medical student and married the seminarian.

In the conversations leading up to the marriage decision, I told my seminarian I loved him, but that I was a lesbian. I hadn't acted on it since high school, I said, but that's how I felt deep down. I liked men too, in that way, well enough, but I felt more connection, more emotional intimacy with women. He would be a lesbian too, then, he said. We would live together like two women would, and we'd work out our roles with no sexism, no roles borrowed from the pa-triarchy. So we married, and for a long time it was pretty good. We had two amazing baby boys, who were a joy. The patriarchal roles are harder to escape than either of us thought, though, and we mostly gave up on shedding them. I worked as a college chap-lain, then as a pastoral counselor. I arranged my practice so that I could spend afternoons with my children.

The Presbyterian context was feeling more and more like

a sweater that I'd outgrown, but I got along well enough because my work was in my counseling office. I couldn't have been a parish minister for the Presbyterians. The slim range of topics I could preach with integrity would have started to set off alarm bells, and the solidity of my doctrine would have been called into question. I would have been outed as someone whose Christianity was unraveling. All I had done was pull on one or two threads of the too-small garment, questioning one or two things, letting go of a couple of certainties, and the whole thing came undone and lay in a pile at my feet, demanding to be knitted into something different, something that fit better. All I had done was explore feminist theology, imagine a female face of God, and the whole idea of God had started to change.

You couldn't just "put Yahweh in drag," as feminist theologian Mary Daly said. Scriptural descriptions of him didn't make sense if he were a mother. Then all I had done was begin to imagine the body and the Earth as sacred, and suddenly the idea that some things were bad and some were good gave way to some being destructive and others life-giving; then it had to be true that some destruction was, eventually, for the good of the whole. If humanity is truly part of the organism of Earth, then what is true for the sea and the trees, the lakes and the lions might also be true for us. Then the whole meaning of "us" changed. Who is included in "us"? Not only did "us" feel like the peoples of the Earth, it began to feel like the water too, and the veldt, and the grasshoppers. This new garment I had to knit together would have to be a whole different shape from the one that had unraveled. What faith could help me do that?

While I was a college chaplain at a small women's college, the local Unitarian Universalist congregation would invite me to speak once a year. I had fun preaching there. "No Presbyterian sermons," the Worship Chair said. "Talk about something that matters to you, or current events, or a poem or a song or something." She didn't have to tell me twice. I was eager to speak from a text other than the Bible, hungry to talk about a broader range of topics. I would sneak peeks at the back of their hymnal. I was astonished by the readings they had put there: poems by Adrienne Rich, Rabindranath Tagore, Mary Oliver, T. S. Eliot. During a dear and funny little segment called Joys and Concerns, members would stand up and share stories about things like seeing a pileated woodpecker in the backyard, or feeling awe and connection on a hike. Most of all, I liked the older folks there. They reminded me of the elderly Quakers I wanted to be like when I used to attend the Haverford Friends Meeting as a teenager. I preached for the Spartanburg congregation through the years of being a college chaplain, then through becoming a pastoral counselor, opening my own business, and becoming the best-known couples counselor in town.

One of my dear friends was a member of the congregation where I would occasionally preach. She and I and two other women, an Episcopalian and a Methodist, met for lunch every Monday for years. We called it "Group." She came in one day and tossed some papers on the table. "Here," she said, "this is your kind of thing." The papers described a conference at The Mountain, in Highlands, North Carolina. There would be drumming and bonfires, dancing and workshops on art and music, creating sacred space, meditation, and other delicious ways to spend time.

"You shouldn't have to go by yourself, so we're all going to go with you."

The four of us signed up and drove to the top of a mountain where, when you looked out over the valley from the porch of your cabin, the hawks flew by far below. The foothills lay as far as the eye could see, like a blanket casually rumpled and let fall. Over the next four days, my three friends watched from a distance, but fondly, as I took to this milieu like a dry oak tree soaking up a good rain. The next spring, I went back to the conference, alone this time, but now surrounded by Unitarian Universalist friends.

More and more, I knew I wanted to change my Presbyterian ordination for a Unitarian Universalist one. I told my husband, who tried to be sympathetic but let me know that having a Unitarian Universalist wife would be hard on his ministerial career. I knew that. I began the process of changing my ordination but kept its pace very, very slow.

Some changes in my life begin with a whisper, like a memory of a time that never was, and I know it means I'm going toward that time that I'm "remembering." Others happen all at once, much less gently, like being hit by a bus. That's how this one happened. Driving back down the mountain from this conference several years later, I tried to process the turn my life had taken the day before. There was a woman, a friend one minute, and the next minute the wind changed, and she was much more to me. It was invisible, having happened only in my own head and heart, this new reality that hit suddenly and hard, but I knew that, no matter what happened with this woman, I would no longer be able to live any longer as heterosexual and married to the Presbyterian minister.

My spirit alternately sang, then sank, back and forth in a dizzying rhythm. What would happen to my children? That was my overriding concern as I drove down into the valley. I began to bargain with the new reality. Maybe I could stick out the marriage. A person didn't have to be 100-percent authentic with every breath of her life. I had worked hard toward that standard, but I could learn to compromise myself just a little. Maybe I could just make the whole thing metaphorical, learn from it. Self-acceptance was the lesson. If I could be this attracted to a woman, it was a celebration of my own womanhood. In what was still a very male-dominated profession, in a family where a large number of people recognized only male ministers, my sense of myself as female had sustained some damage. Yes, I was going to look at this attraction as a healing, not as love for another woman. I would not embarrass my children, not rip my life to shreds, not become something many people around me found abhorrent, something with which my family would struggle, not ruin my business as well as my marriage.

I tried that for a year or two. You can imagine how well it worked. Finally, I told my husband I needed to live authentically, and that meant coming out as a lesbian. "I thought you were becoming a Unitarian," he said, and we both laughed. That was the last laugh we shared for a long time.

It was hard to gauge which would cause a greater scandal in our town, which would cause my family more distress. As we ended the marriage, we tried to be the best parents we could be to the boys, who adjusted to joint custody pretty well. I looked around for something to supplement my counseling practice since I'd made myself let go of all the couples work while my marriage ended. It so happened that, at that same time, the Unitarian Universalist church in our town asked if I would consider being their interim minister. They knew I was in the process of changing over my ordination. I accepted with delight. The Presbyterian administration for that district disapproved of my new job. They called me in and told me I would have to "lay down" my ordination. The Unitarian Universalists told me they would catch it before it hit the ground and that they'd be proud to have me.

I still hadn't come out in public. I didn't want my boys to suffer at school. I felt that the church leaders deserved to know, however, and I thought and pondered about how to tell them. At a board meeting, I asked that we go into executive session. I told them, and they were lovely about it. They were surprised that they were ending up with someone a bit different from the woman they thought they'd hired, but one gay board member told me I shouldn't go around coming out to people, expecting they would be happy about it. "It's not good news to everyone," he said. Good news? What planet did he live on? It wasn't good news to anyone I knew. If I could have made it go away, I would have. The discussion ended and we came out of executive session.

"What should I write about this in the minutes?" the board secretary asked.

"We went into executive session, . . ." one person began.

And then a tall wiry man in his seventies, a pillar of Unitarian Universalism nationwide, said, "And then we came out!"

What I knew about my town was this: If I ducked my head in shame even a little, the other chickens in the yard would peck me to death. The best-known couples' counselor in town had just ended her marriage. One of the favorite local adult education teachers, having taught at the Presbyterian, Methodist, and Episcopal churches, had just come out as a Unitarian Universalist. Most people knew I was gay. Moving to another town wasn't an option. The boys needed me and they needed their dad close by. All their friends and mine were here. I had to hold my head high and deal. I rented a yellow house in a downtown neighborhood where nearly all of the town's "pillars" lived.

It was right behind the best elementary school in town. I said hello to everyone at the grocery store. Only a few of them turned their backs to me without speaking. I went to the kids' basketball games at the church where their dad was the minister. Only a few of the people turned their backs to me without speaking.

The Unitarian Universalist church gave me a place to stand. My boys and I threw ourselves into life there and got through those first two years. When the interim ended, I went back to my counseling practice and worked part-time in the office of a friend who was helping local industries be more ecologically sound. We laughed every day at work. I had my guitar by my desk and got to know lots of folks who worked with their hands and their backs as well as their brains. They knew I was gay and it didn't seem to matter.

After four years, the church was open again. They did a search and I got the job. Settled ministry felt very different from interim ministry, but I liked it very much too. Being in my "right livelihood" felt wonderful.

Over the years, I was impressed by how little trouble I was given personally because of my sexuality. My partner and I would go to restaurants with our mixed brood. Two fair boys and two coffee-colored girls with two moms. You could tell people were wondering what the story was. When I had to deal with the healthcare system, and I was on my partner's insurance, no one blinked. They would ask, "Married? Divorced?" I would say, "Partnered." They made another space on the form and wrote it in. We never had problems with visitation, and we were treated like a couple more in the healthcare system in that small southern town than anywhere else.

All around, though, preachers railed against homosexuality. Earnest and principled people threw their own gay children out of their homes in order to "wake them up" to the seriousness of their souls' danger. They were responsible for the eternal destination of their children's souls, after all, so they fought tooth and nail to "save" their kids from themselves. I heard terrible stories of exorcisms, street life, beatings. A sweet man told me his dad let him know that he thought everything bad that had happened to their family over the years was because his son's gayness had "torn down the hedge of God's protection" around the family. One story was terrible and funny at the same time: A man in his twenties told a group of us how his mom, finding out he was gay, called in a minister named Rev. Feely to come lay hands on him. We had the same gallows humor that anyone gets when they hear and see too many terrible things, I guess.

There in the middle of all of that distress, guilt, and condemnation stood the Unitarian Universalists. Not a perfect refuge, of course, but nonetheless, a lifesaving one. In that small town, the Unitarian Universalist church started Coming Out Day celebrations, including a sermon about homosexuality and the Bible, a panel of folks advertised as "ask a gay person anything," and a Coming Out Coffeehouse, where every year seventy to eighty gay and straight people danced and celebrated at the church. Some years later, two straight women from that church helped organize the first Pride March in the town. The mayor asked them not to do it. Police were deployed in preparation for a terrible backlash. More than 400 people, black, white, Asian, all genders and orientations, came out to march. Forty protesters shouted that we were going to hell, but we just sang louder and drowned out the condemnation. The next year, 1,500 people marched. That congregation changed Spartanburg, South Carolina.

Even in the midst of places where homophobia is less accepted, the Unitarian Universalist congregations stand as places where most of the people, most of the time, want a world where gay folks are as integrated into the fabric of society as anyone else. That world is a long way off, but sometimes I can see it from our Unitarian Universalist congregations.

―◦―

MEG BARNHOUSE *grew up in North Carolina and Philadelphia, and has lived in Spartanburg, South Carolina, since 1981. After graduating from Duke University and Princeton*

Theological Seminary, she worked as chaplain to Converse College for six years, teaching public speaking, human sexuality, and world religions. She helped found the SAFE Homes Network for battered women in her community. Credentialed as a Fellow in the American Association of Pastoral Counselors, she retains a small private pastoral counseling practice while serving as full-time minister of the Unitarian Universalist Church of Spartanburg. She travels nationwide as a speaker, singer-songwriter, and humorist. Meg is the mother of two sons, ages eighteen and twenty-one. She has a second-degree black belt in karate. She is a commentator for North Carolina Public Radio on the program "Radio Free Bubba" and has also been heard on National Public Radio's "Weekend All Things Considered." Her many books are compilations of her radio stories, and she has also produced CDs of original songs and stories.

THE LONG ROAD HOME

ANNETTE MARQUIS

I guess you could say that my coming out as a lesbian was a religious experience. It was 1973. I had just turned eighteen and was in my senior year at a Roman Catholic boarding school when I was outed to my parents—by a nun. Sister Anne expressed her concern to me that I was ruining my reputation. She then called my mother and reported that I was involved in an "unsavory" relationship with another girl in my class. This was not welcome news to my devout Catholic parents.

From my mother's perspective, I might have been born with this affliction. She firmly believed my homosexuality was a punishment from God for her transgressions. I don't know what caused my homosexuality. What I do know is that, from my earliest memory, I wanted to be a boy. I dressed as a boy, liked boys' games, and took the role of a boy in the play-acting we did as children. From a very young age, I was recognized by others as someone with both male and female characteristics. My second-grade teacher, Sister Mary Letitia, cast me to play the owl in a dramatic version of the Edward Lear classic children's poem, "The Owl and the Pussycat." Everyone, including me, assumed Owl was the male-identified character who was in love with the lovely female Pussycat.

In fourth grade, I distinctly remember my mother asking, "Why do you always have your arms around all the other little girls?" She had come to pick me up at the end of the day, and posed the question as soon as I climbed into our family's 1963 Chevy Impala station wagon. I shrugged it off at the time. "I don't know," I mumbled, but from that day forward, I was much more aware of my physical contact with other girls.

By the time I was an adolescent, I knew I didn't fit in. All the girls in my class were dating boys, and when

they weren't out with them, they were talking about them. I couldn't relate. I proposed to my parents that they send me to a Catholic boarding school in Michigan—where Sister Anne eventually outed me.

I have often wondered what might have happened if Sister Anne hadn't forced me to give a name to the behavior I was engaged in, hadn't caused me to go to the public library to surreptitiously read about homo-sexuality, hadn't triggered my desire to explore my identity. By the time I made it to college, I was relieved to find other women like me. Although no one talked openly about it, lesbians made up the bulk of the women's basketball team. To be in my first community of lesbians was energizing, affirming, and most important, enlightening.

I became a sponge for anything I could find about lesbians. I was in a friend's dorm room one day when I saw *Sappho Was a Right-On Woman* on her bookshelf. My heart started racing, my palms got sweaty, and I knew I had to read that book. I finally screwed up my courage and took the plunge. "Can I, um, borrow that, um, book about, um, Sappho?" I asked sheepishly. Lisa laughed, "It's not about Sappho. It's about us. Of course, you can borrow it." *Sappho Was a Right-On Woman* is one of the very first books written by lesbians about lesbians, and it launched my journey into a whole new world of lesbian culture.

I was inspired by the lesbian liberation movement described in Del Martin and Phyllis Lyon's self-published book, *Lesbian Woman*. Del and Phyllis became my heroes. They taught me about the courage it took to be an activist, an organizer, and a pioneer. By publishing *The Ladder*, the first national lesbian periodical, they showed me the importance of connecting with other lesbians. As the first lesbian couple to join the National Organization for Women, they taught me the value of making ourselves visible in nongay organizations. And on June 16, 2008, fifty-six years into their relationship, when Del and Phyllis became the first same-sex couple to be legally married in San Francisco, I celebrated their union as if my own grandmothers were getting married.

My college chaplain, Father John Kiefer, was the first person I ever heard refer to "Mother and Father God." It wasn't long after that I discovered Mary Daly, once described by the *New York Times Book Review* as a "controversial radical feminist philosopher, theologian, mythologist, explorer, pirate, warrior, witch, fairy and leprechaun." I devoured her books *The Church and the Second Sex* and *Beyond God the Father* and was introduced to a theology quite different from the one that I had been raised on. Daly's theology opened the door for me to think about God not as a white-haired, bearded man in the sky but as a life force for all that is good and holy. This life force could not be defined by gender any more than wind or rain could be.

Soon after graduation, I stopped attending church. At school, I had the benefit of a few liberal-minded nuns and a college chaplain who saw women as his equals. Outside the school environment, I realized that if the Church could not respect me as a woman, it certainly was not going to accept me as a lesbian. After I left, I explored Goddess spirituality, feminist theology, paganism, Wicca, Native American spirituality, earth- and nature-based spiritualities, liberation theology, New Age spirituality, and a host of other forms of spiritual expression. But no matter how hard I tried, I didn't find the religious home I was seeking. The closest I came was in adopting Native American spirituality. In this tradition, I found rituals that grounded me and a theology that honored the sacredness of life. However, as I became aware of the pain caused by cultural misappropriation, I knew I could not claim these sacred traditions as my own.

Although still feeling spiritually bereft, I was beginning to embrace my lesbian identity. Through the help of a therapist, I came to own labels such as *lesbian*, *dyke*, and *butch*. I gave up on my feeble attempts to be "normal" and started to find power in my differences. At every opportunity, I fought against standard gender roles and the male oppression of women. I became radicalized, eventually finding my way to radical lesbian separatism.

During that time, I lived a bifurcated existence. In my work life, I was a human services professional, working for the patriarchy while hiding my lesbianism and trying not to appear too extreme in my feminist ideology. Outside work, I lived in a woman-identified world, isolated from men as much as possible. I socialized only with women. I devoured feminist and lesbian publications. I became involved in lesbian political action groups. And I listened almost exclusively to woman's music, a genre of music created by Cris Williamson, Meg Christian, Holly Near, Heather Bishop, and Margie Adam, who inspired, educated, and comforted me in my struggle for women's and lesbian liberation.

At the same time, I couldn't fully embrace the ideals of the radical lesbian feminists who called for the creation of a woman-only society. My annual pilgrimage to the Michigan Womyn's Music Festival, a gathering of from 5,000 to 12,000 women that began in 1975, was the closest I came to adopting the separatist life offered by radical lesbian feminists. "Welcome home," a woman said as she greeted each car passing through the gates to "the Land." And I was at home there.

The Land offered me a vision of what a feminist society might look like. It was by no means perfect. But it was different enough that I glimpsed the world I wanted to work toward—a multicultural world that provides for the differently abled, the elderly, and those affected by addictions and chemical sensitivities, a world where music and the arts are treasured, where people's skills are respected, where children are treated as human beings, and where people live in peaceful community in harmony with nature.

When I returned to work each year after the festival, I returned to the closet. Because I hadn't found the courage to be out as a lesbian in the world of patriarchy or the courage to leave patriarchy behind, I hid out in both worlds. The conflict caused me to search constantly—for a different job, a different geographic location, something that would make me spiritually, emotionally, and intellectually whole.

Sitting at a women's coffeehouse in the basement of the Unitarian Universalist Church of Flint, Michigan, one Saturday evening in 1991, I said to my life partner, "I hear they have a cool lesbian minister at this church. Maybe we should go check the place out tomorrow." My partner's assent might have lacked enthusiasm, but it was all I needed. I don't remember arriving at church that first Sunday, how we were greeted, where we sat, what the sermon was about, or who talked with us afterwards. All I remember is I wanted to go back.

Unitarian Universalism was not new to either of us. My partner's father was a Unitarian minister. For ten years, I had heard countless stories about the formation of the Unitarian Universalist Association, Meadville Lombard Theological School, and all the parishes her father had served. But we did not go to church. In my partner's eyes, no minister could live up to the standards set by her father. Since I still thought of myself as a refugee from the Catholic Church, I had not brought up the idea of attending church.

Something changed the day we attended that service at the Unitarian Universalist Church of Flint. Maybe it was the lesbian minister—I know I would not have gone if she hadn't been there. Maybe it was the brokenness I felt, living such a fragmented life. Maybe it was my growing need for spiritual community. Maybe it was the breath of the Holy Spirit. I don't know what it was for sure, but something drew me in and captured my soul.

What astounded me was that I could be out as a lesbian and we could be out as a couple in a predominantly straight environment. We could go to church, hold hands, and share our lives in a public way. It was transformational. My world got a whole lot bigger. It now included men, boy children, and transsexuals. The church pianist, for example, was a male-to-female transsexual who, after years of attending the Michigan Womyn's Music Festival, found herself barred when it was announced that only "womyn born womyn" were welcome. This began to illuminate for me in a very personal way how separatism was not the answer, could not be the answer, if the Beloved Community I longed for was to become real.

Transitioning from a life in which I rarely chose the company of men to one in which I was inviting men in was not easy for me. I raised my doubts with the minister a few months after I started attending the church: "I don't know if I can become a member. I thought that finally giving up my identity as a Catholic would be hard. And it is. But the biggest challenge for me is choosing to be a part of an organization where I will need to work with men." Much to my surprise, the minister didn't recoil at my intolerance; she listened to my concerns and helped me explore them from a spiritual perspective.

It took me nearly a year to decide to join the congregation. I still had some trepidation, but I held on to a vision of Beloved Community and took the leap. I found that the support of a spiritual community gave me the courage to come out in my work life. And even though my growing commitment to Unitarian Universalism ultimately resulted in the loss of my relationship with my partner, I was an integrated, whole woman, living a life consistent with my values for the first time. I was free.

There are still times when I need to be in lesbian-only space in order to renew my spirit and feel ready to engage again. Fortunately, I have been able to meet that need both inside and outside my faith community. It is in these respites that I am able to most plainly see the great progress we have made as Unitarian Universalists, and the work we still need to do.

I have been a Unitarian Universalist for nineteen years. In that time, I have seen us grow dramatically in our acceptance of lesbian and gay people and, to a lesser extent, those who are bisexual and transgender. In most congregations, being gay is no big deal. More than two-thirds of congregations are designated by the Unitarian Universalist Association (UUA) as Welcoming Congregations to lesbian, gay, bisexual, transgender, and queer/questioning people. In theory, and often in practice, LGBTQ people are integrated into the life of the community. But that doesn't mean the work is done.

When a congregation "accepts" me but is not actively engaged in efforts to fight discrimination against LGBTQ people, I feel as if I'm being told, "It's alright that you're gay, but don't talk about it too much. Act like us and you'll be accepted here just fine." What many well-intentioned heterosexual people forget is that I can't just leave my sexual orientation at the door. Because I don't have a mark on my forehead or a pink triangle sewn into my sleeve, I make a conscious choice with everyone I meet whether or not I will come out to them. Do I have to change pronouns from "she" to "he" if I make small talk with the hairstylist about my upcoming wedding? Is it dangerous if my new neighbors find out I'm a lesbian? Am I copping out if I don't accept a Facebook friend request from an old family friend who doesn't know about my personal life? Coming out is never a one-time event, it is a daily practice. And it can be exhausting.

Even within Unitarian Universalism, I evaluate every situation to determine if I want to take the risk of exposing my full self. I have preached on civil rights, on antiracism, and on the general topic of oppression on multiple occasions. But fifteen years passed after I became a Unitarian Universalist lay leader, and three years after I became a member of the UUA staff, before I agreed to preach on LGBTQ issues. I told myself that I didn't want to push my personal agenda on anyone. Truth be told, speaking out on LGBTQ issues just hits too close to home for me. I fought for my rights and dignity for decades before I became a Unitarian Universalist. I don't want to have to do that all over again in my faith community.

For me to feel certain a congregation is serious about its commitment to being welcoming, I look for two things. First, I look for the congregation to be actively working to change unfair laws on local, state, national, and/or international levels. I see that they regularly speak out against discrimination in their communities and support attempts to secure civil rights for LGBTQ people. Second, I look to see that they are teaching their members how to be more accepting and more inclusive of LGBTQ people in their lives.

Changing laws, policies, and practices that discriminate against LGBTQ people is essential work for our congregations. Discrimination in employment, housing, military service, education, adoption, immigration, and marriage continues to affect LGBTQ people every day. Congregations can choose to embrace this work in many different ways. If, for example, a congregation has a history of outreach to the military, it can focus on supporting LGBTQ people who, since the 2010 repeal of "Don't Ask, Don't Tell," are adjusting to living openly in the military; or it can reach out to LGBTQ service people who were discharged under this discriminatory law. If a congregation is doing work on immigration, it can work to assure that LGBTQ people are treated fairly under U.S. immigration laws. If a congregation is working on issues of homelessness in its community, it can examine issues around homeless LGBTQ youth.

LGBTQ youth make up the single highest percentage of homeless youth in this country, and their plight is an issue near to my heart. In the early 1990s, the Unitarian Universalist Congregation of Grand Traverse in Traverse City, Michigan, partnered with a local mental health crisis center to start a weekly support group for LGBTQ youth. When I served as executive director of the crisis center several years later, I personally experienced Unitarian Universalist community ministry at work. Children's lives were saved through this simple outreach.

Many of these issues and others are addressed in the UUA's public advocacy campaign called Standing on the Side of Love. Standing on the Side of Love seeks to harness love's power to stop oppression wherever it is found. This campaign is an exciting new way for congregations to draw attention to the legal discrimination confronting LGBTQ people in committed relationships, protections most heterosexual people take for granted, such as the right to marry; make medical decisions for their spouses; be covered by spouses' health, retirement, and pension plans; and receive social security, inheritance, and other tax benefits. First Unitarian Universalist Church of Richmond, Virginia, for example, sponsors an annual Valentine's Day action in which a number of same-sex couples apply for marriage licenses at the city courthouse. This type of action makes it clear to LGBTQ people that the congregation is serious about its commitment to end discrimination.

It's also important to recognize that congregations have an impact on the lives of LGBTQ people through their internal policies and practices. A congregation's commitment to welcome LGBTQ people must permeate every program, every service, every decision that the congregation makes. Does the congregation, for example, have a way to accommodate same-sex couples who want to pledge as a family but need separate tax statements? Are forms, such as membership or wedding application forms, inclusive of same-sex couples? Are transgender people invited to be greeters on Sunday mornings? By evaluating its own practices, a congregation can make a difference in the lives of LGBTQ people even as it confronts larger societal issues.

Changing laws or policies alone, however, isn't going to end discrimination. To do so, we need to touch people's hearts. That's one of the reasons my wife, Wendy, and I chose to get married in our Unitarian Universalist church in Virginia. Even though our marriage isn't legally recognized in Virginia, we chose to declare our love in front of family, friends, coworkers, and members of our congregation—witnesses, straight and gay alike—and invite them to become part of our commitment to each other. What a gift it was to have the ceremony officiated by two Unitarian Universalist ministers we love and respect! "By the power vested in us by the Unitarian Universalist Association and this congregation, we now pronounce you spouses for life," they said in unison at the end of the service. Their life-affirming words recall our faith's Puritan roots. As Rev. Rebecca Parker has written, "Our Puritan forbears resisted oppression by putting into practice a way of life that manifested an alternative to the structures of oppression that dominated their lives. This was the heart of their covenant: to be what they wanted to see, to live as if the day of justice had arrived." Our wed-

ding was, for us, an act of creating the future. On that day, we lived as if justice for LGBTQ people had arrived.

In order to move us even closer to that day, we asked one more thing of our guests: that they share the experience of our wedding with others. We asked them, as our straight friends and family members, to come out with us, to find the courage to make us a visible part of their lives. We asked them to talk openly with coworkers, friends, and families about the LGBTQ people they know and love—to freely share photos from our wedding, tell stories about the wonderful Thanksgiving dinner they had with their lesbian daughter and her family, or talk about how upset they are that their brother can't get domestic partner benefits for his husband where he works.

This is the true meaning of standing on the side of love: doing the work of changing people's hearts and minds. It is also the work of our congregations and the Unitarian Universalist Association: to challenge us to live by our shared principles and highest ideals in order to create a Beloved Community here on earth.

◄o►

ANNETTE MARQUIS *calls herself a ricochet Southerner, born in the North, raised in the West and then the South, educated in the North and the East, and now happily living back in the Southeast. She became a Unitarian Universalist in 1991 and almost immediately became active as a lay leader in her congregation, the district, and the Unitarian Universalist Association* *at large. She was one of the founding members of Unitarian Universalist Allies for Racial Equity and served as its chair for its first two years. She served as a JUUST Change consultant and a Beyond Categorical Thinking trainer for the UUA. As a volunteer for Unitarian Universalist Trauma Response Ministry, Annette provided mental health and other disaster relief to victims of Hurricane Katrina. She has served in her present capacity as district executive of the Thomas Jefferson District of the Unitarian Universalist Association since 2006. Annette currently lives in Richmond, Virginia, with her wife, Wendy, where together they enjoy women's basketball, hiking, writing, and new technology.*

Growing into Alignment

Meg Riley

In 1977, at age twenty-two, I read Mary Daly's book *Beyond God the Father: Toward a Philosophy of Women's Liberation* (published by the Unitarian Universalist-founded Beacon Press). It is impossible to state, more than thirty years later, the profoundly radical meaning that this book held for me. By the time I finished, I realized that theology was more interesting to me than anything else in the world, and that I was a lesbian. "The unfolding of God, then, is an event in which women participate as we participate in our own revolution. The process involves the creation of new space, in which women are free to become who we are."

Of course, I think now, it had to be a book, not a human encounter, that finally clarified my sexual orientation. Somebody more in her body might have noticed some things years earlier. How I fell apart when my "close friends" fell in love with men. How I found something wrong with every man who expressed interest in me. How I loved flannel shirts, overalls, and close-cropped hair—in myself and in others. I used to say to friends, in bewilderment, "If I were a lesbian, my life would make more sense . . . but I'm not!" In retrospect, I think a self-protective instinct kept me unconscious of my deepest desires till I was twenty-two. The radical reframing of ultimate meaning by Mary Daly, who could name what kept women from being liberated and who encouraged women to create new time and new space, literally gave me permission to know what I had always known, to feel my own body sensations, and to become congruent with them.

So there I was, on the brink of coming out and also wondering in what way I might pursue this new interest in theology. I had grown up Unitarian Universalist but hadn't gone to church since I'd left my parents' congregation after high school. I sought and found a congregation five blocks down the street from my post-college cooperative house and went to visit. The preacher used poetry in a way I found life giving. I approached him, explaining that I was trying to figure out how to sort through these two epiphanies. He invited me to his house one night to talk about it. And then this middle-aged married man put the moves on me. I don't remember the details, only shouting "No!" over my shoulder to his offer of a ride home as I ran out the door into a pretornado green sky and wild rain, the sirens blaring as I panted and grunted and ran and cried. Drenched by my tears and the wild rain, inseparable from each other, I ran into my house and shut myself into my room, still sobbing. I backed away not only from this minister but from Unitarian Universalism and, thus, all church.

After that, I did lesbian total immersion for a while. Though history records the late seventies and early eighties as a time of narcissism, it was a time of profound depth and exploration for feminists, queers, and freethinkers.

In South Minneapolis, where I moved because that's where the lesbians were, we were recreating the way we thought, talked, dreamed, lived, ate, worked, loved, got ourselves around, and created families. An old friend visiting said that he had never heard anyone use the word *power* as often I did in one conversation. I lived in a lesbian co-op house, danced in a group called Lesbian Moves, cooked in a breakfast collective called LezEat, and volunteered at a lesbian newspaper called *The Lesbian Inciter*. Ten of us rented a farm together and then a camp on a lake. We took poetry classes and studied Adrienne Rich and Audre Lorde with a brave, boldly out lesbian professor. I joined a lesbian empowerment group. We created Goddess-centered rituals for every occasion. Every Friday and Saturday night, we danced to disco in the basement of Plymouth Congregational Church, after hearing performances by local women playing their own songs or those of lesbian singer-songwriters like Meg Christian and Cris Williamson.

We put a lesbian sensibility on everything. Come August, we went to the Michigan Womyn's Music Festival, where thousands of women went naked and listened to feminist music for a solid week. It was total immersion, although I never called myself a separatist. My former friends and family were bewildered and bored. I was re-creating myself, becoming a lesbian cell by cell. Another old friend, visiting, said in bewilderment after hearing me rant for a while, "OK, I get that you are passionate, but explain to me what it has to do with the mayor of Chicago?" No, no, not Mayor Daley, Mary Daly!

Three years or so later, I realized I was becoming claustrophobic in my lesbian enclave. I considered my options and decided to attend seminary. At the time, I planned to be a religious educator. Midway through seminary, in 1985, I became the director of religious education at a large Unitarian Universalist church. The dream job I had thought I might get years later was already mine in my late twenties

I never meant to be in the closet. But six weeks after I arrived, the longstanding senior minister gave notice, and I didn't know where to garner the support I needed to come out, especially as a young novice DRE. I had never met a gay or lesbian minister. This was twenty-five years ago! I loved my work, but I entered that strange, genderless-pronoun, detail-free world of the closeted. What did you do on the weekend? Hung out with friends in the country. Translation: Ten of us had a huge party at the lake to celebrate my fifth anniversary with my partner. I led two lives, still participating in the lesbian community fully—including the new, mostly closeted, gay and lesbian friends of all faiths I was meeting in seminary—and going to church as a competent, friendly, professional—and partial—self.

Adrienne Rich tells us that "what is unspoken becomes unspeakable." During those two years of silence, my car got totaled one day as I left the church. I was two feet from being dead. The Board president also happened to be leaving the church and saw the wreck. Completely rattled, I gratefully accepted the board president's hug, and we stood in shock as the tow trucks arrived and hauled away the scrap metal that had been my car. At that moment, my partner showed up. Did I leave his embrace and go to her? No. Having nearly been killed, I nodded almost imperceptibly to her as if I were an eighth grader and she my parent picking me up from my soccer game.

After I'd been at the church for a while, a lay leader stopped in my office and, in a conversational tone, said to me, "Am I crazy, or are you a lesbian?" My heart pounding, I stammered out, "You're . . . not . . . crazy!" Not noticing my terror, she went on breezily, "Well, I thought so. I mean, you totally seem like a lesbian. The first week you were here, I noted to the board how great it was that now we had a gay music director and a lesbian RE director!" As she went on, my own brain was riveted: the first week I was there? All of my stumbling around and stuttering, and no one had ever said anything to me for two years, even though they had discussed my sexual orientation *the first week I was there?!*

Consider what this revelation meant: Nearly dead, I did not reach for the comfort offered by my own partner. This is how deep the closet goes. To learn that the board president knew, from week one, that I was a lesbian makes the loss in that story doubly painful to recount.

I have been on the other side of that closet and know the pain from there. A colleague, so clearly gay it never occurred to me he didn't think himself completely out, had a friend who got AIDS in the early nineties. Over and over I asked him, "How is your friend?" Only when the friend died and my colleague fell apart, did I understand that this "friend" had been his partner, and that he was not telling us that meaningful fact because he thought we didn't know he was gay and would reject him if we did.

In 1991, when my then-partner and I had a union ceremony, her Catholic mother immediately responded to our invitation with a letter that began, "My grieving will never end." My own Unitarian Universalist parents didn't respond at all. Not a word. We had timed the invitation to arrive a week before we visited them for a weekend—all weekend, not a word. As we were pulling out of the drive to leave, my mother said, "You said you liked that vase—do you want it for a gift at your union ceremony?" I was stunned. "You're—coming—then?" "Well, of course!" she said, as if this total silence were normal. That's liberal homophobia. Personally, I find overt expressions of discomfort easier to deal with. Because it is named and claimed, you know where you are.

Liberal silence—even in the name of respecting other people's right not to say anything if they don't want to—can be as oppressive as hostility. In the face of silence, we each invent our own monsters. We assume that others' perceptions are the same as our negative judgments about ourselves. I say this because so much has changed since then. It is important to name how it was. My own mother went through such profound transformation about homophobia at her church that she became a surrogate mom and advocate to many other LGBT people. I remember her calling me after going to an election event where Hillary Clinton had spoken in 1996. She left a message: In front of her at the rally was a lesbian couple with a baby from China! (My partner and I were then in the process of adoption.) I called her back: "How was she?" I asked, meaning Hillary. "Adorable!" she responded, confusing me until I remembered she was behaving like any soon-to-be grandmother.

My mother's minister, who came out while serving that church, told me later that on the Sunday when she gathered her courage to tell the congregation about her new life, my mother leapt up early in the service during joys and concerns to wave around photos we had just received from China, squealing, "I'm going to be a grandmother!" with nothing but joy. The minister said that a church leader so excited about having a lesbian daughter who was in a relationship and planning to be a parent helped her relax.

So how do we step out of those old closets that shape us so deeply that we can look into the face of death and still stay in them? I have had dozens of healing experiences within Unitarian Universalism, for which I am eternally grateful.

In 1989, I became the youth programs director at the Unitarian Universalist Association (UUA). Determined not to re-enter the closet, I came out immediately during my interview. By 1989, dozens of gay and lesbian and bisexual staff had already blazed the UUA trails that I would walk on. It truly was a nonissue. Not the kind of nonissue that means, "We don't want to hear about that." My sexuality was the kind of nonissue that means, "We *do* want to hear about your life, just like anyone else's." What a relief! The youth, in particular, were interested, supportive, curious.

I helped plan and facilitate a Liberal Religious Educators Association meeting, called The Welcoming LREDA, named to reflect the UUA's Welcoming Congregation program that began in 1989. After several days of profound sharing and listening, we began moving in a closing circle, singing the Libby Roderick song, "How Could Anyone?": "How could

anyone ever tell you you were anything less than beautiful? / How could anyone ever tell you you were less than whole?" Moving slowly in that circle, I became so overwhelmed with the relief of clear, honest connection with this community of religious leaders that I began, to my own shock, sobbing deeply. Soon a group of us huddled together in the center of that moving circle, clutching one another and bawling. When the song ended, and we looked at one another, I realized that the front of my shirt was as drenched as it had been those years earlier in the tornado-threatened streets. "It gives new meaning to the phrase *wet t-shirt*, doesn't it?" observed a droll older white male minister, as soaked as I was.

I was director of the Unitarian Universalist Office of Lesbian, Bisexual and Gay Concerns in 1992, when homophobic ballot initiatives threatened the people of Colorado and Oregon. I woke up then to the fact that, as imperfect as Unitarian Universalism might be in our response to oppression or exclusion related to gender or sexual orientation, we were light years ahead of the rest of the religious communities, and we needed to step out.

That was when my selves began to come into closer alignment. That wild-eyed radical young dyke from my early twenties was now able not only to talk about but actually claim her power—as a minister, as a public speaker, stepping out and challenging this oppressive view of religion. I flew out of the doors of Unitarian Universalist churches and began to speak anywhere and everywhere I could, to interfaith and secular audiences, about the homophobia of the religious right. I wasn't much fun at a party right then, but I was on fire with a mission. Ironically, my own theological clarity about oppression and what is holy emerged in this public forum. You have to keep it so simple with media, and I heard myself saying over and over such things as:

We are all created in God's image. Our love is a gift from God, who is love. The only way God's love can be felt here on earth is through us, so we deny that gift at the peril of ourselves and the world.

Once a hostile, right-wing TV pundit said to me, "Unitarians don't think *anything* is a sin, do you?" I responded, "We believe that homophobia, not homosexuality, is a sin." Standing on the Side of Love, the UUA's public advocacy campaign against oppression, now provides wallet cards emblazoned with that affirmation. In a sermon for Unitarian Universalists, I will parse the word *God* for the nervous ones. In public, I picture that one suicidal teenager and keep it just as simple as I can. "God is Love. Love is God."

As I look back on my ministry, I can see the evolution of my own conviction that I have something of value to offer the world. At first, I could only imagine that I was safe offering it to kids, then teens, then queers or queer allies, then social justice activists. Now I feel confident that the path I have walked is relevant and meaningful, not just to subsets of people but for the good of the whole world. It has been my blessing to receive strong support from our religious movement throughout my evolution. I wish similar support for every person.

Recently, I realized that my center of meaning and support has shifted from lesbian feminism to a much broader faith perspective. I left the daily shelter of that lesbian enclave more than twenty years ago to go to seminary. Now my network of grounding and support is truly located in the ocean, not the stream or the river. Sure, there are moments when I want another "queer eye" so we can raise our queer eyebrows at each other. But on a daily basis, I feel that I have access to everything, not just a tiny fraction of life that is safe for me. I have access to existential courage and faith in ways I couldn't have dreamed of in my twenties.

May future generations of queers take their value as human beings for granted and use that value to create more life.

◄o►

MEG RILEY *is the senior minister of the Church of the Larger Fellowship, an online Unitarian Universalist congregation. Prior to assuming that position, she served at the Unitarian Universalist Association's national headquarters for twenty-one years in a variety of roles, including, for a time, as the director of the Office of LGBT Concerns. Riley is founding board chair of Faith in Public Life: A Resource Center for Justice and the Common Good. Previously, she has served on the boards of the Religious Coalition for Reproductive Choice, Americans United for Separation of Church and State, Interfaith Worker Justice, and the Interfaith Alliance. She is a regular blogger on the* Huffington Post *and a columnist on Pathos.com. Riley lives with her family in South Minneapolis.*

LESBIAN MINISTER

JONALU JOHNSTONE

I never set out to be a "lesbian minister." Sure, I wanted to be a minister. And as a Unitarian Universalist, I assumed my sexual orientation wouldn't be an issue. The little congregation I belonged to—Unitarian Universalist Fellowship of Greater Cumberland (Maryland)—had supported me as I gradually came out to myself, and then to others, during the 1980s. I attended my first Interweave Convocation as a layperson, invited by another congregation member. I had read the positions of the Unitarian Universalist Association that are supportive of people like me. At Harvard Divinity School, where I got my degree for ministry, we were able to proudly proclaim our sexuality, even protesting the commencement speaker, Gen. Colin Powell, with pink anti-"Don't Ask, Don't Tell" balloons. My presence in my internship congregation helped to precipitate a pretty fabulous experience of helping the First Unitarian Church of Reading, Massachusetts, to become a

Welcoming Congregation. It was wonderful to see the gay and lesbian people there begin to find one another and, especially, to feel the support of people who actually gave their minister, Rev. Jane Rzepka, a standing ovation for a progay sermon.

So, I was taken aback when I began my ministerial search in the nineties and realized that some congregations were simply not interested in gay or lesbian—much less bisexual or transgender—professionals in leadership.

One colleague told the story of how everything went smoothly in early discussions with an interested congregation—at first. She thought she had been clear in her packet about her sexual orientation by mentioning her affiliation with bisexual, gay, lesbian, and transgender-affirming groups. Until she directly came out to them, however, the search committee had been clueless. And once they realized her sexual orientation, she slid off their list of possible ministers.

I was luckier. I found a congregation that not only embraced my sexuality but was thrilled with it. The James Reeb Unitarian Universalist Church (JRUUC) was not real yet, more a dream and vision that originated with the First Unitarian Society in Madison, Wisconsin, which had set out to spawn a new congregation. The organizing committee in place when I arrived included lesbians, and they were eager to reach out to the East Side, which included a part of town my local contacts called "Dyke Heights." Madison, in fact, had been the lesbian mecca in the 1980s to me and my friends in West Virginia. We had heard stories of this almost mythic place where lesbian feminists moved to feel comfortable and secure. No wonder JRUUC was pleased and proud to have the chance to bring a real live lesbian on board as their first minister.

I came to the position at JRUUC not through a traditional ministerial search but through the Extension Department. I never entered a full search, in part because of discouraging reports I heard from other gay and lesbian ministers, but more because I was genuinely excited by the prospect of creating something new. I had been a charter member of one congregation and a member of a small lay-led congregation, so I felt I had some background for being the first minister of a congregation. I had entered the Extension Ministry Program, which at that time helped to match ministers with congregations that had never had ministry before. The ministers—many of them newly minted—had a week of intensive training before beginning their ministries, and subsequent annual gatherings to reflect on their specialized positions and learn more.

When I remember those gatherings, I am reminded of how many gay and lesbian clergy began their ministries there. Perhaps established congregations would have called these talented people, or at least some of them. Or maybe they would have passed them over, not wanting to rock the boat with someone whose sexuality might end up raising eyebrows. The head of the Extension Department, Rev. Charles Gaines, deserves credit for greatly speeding the opening of opportunities to gay and lesbian ministers through his appointments to these congregations. Many of us proved ourselves in extension congregations.

Ordained only a month before by my proud lay-led home congregation, I arrived in Madison during the summer of 1993, ready to start a church with the help of an organizing committee, strong support—including money—from First Unitarian Society, and a grant from the Extension Department.

It didn't take long before I was known as the "lesbian minister" in town.

To be fair, within my congregation, my identity never narrowly proscribed my role. Within the church, lesbian was part of who I was. I did the same things that any minister would do: preach, teach, visit hospitals and jail, organize committees, meet with the Board, dedicate children, help raise money. The differences came primarily in how I related to and was perceived by the rest of the community, where the lesbian identity seemed to supersede all else.

Being a lesbian minister shaped and changed my ministry in at least three ways: a strong identification of JRUUC as lesbian-friendly, development of a public-witness

ministry centered on LGBT issues, and an opportunity to
minister to and learn from communities I might never
have encountered.

JRUUC had lesbians involved even in its organizing
phase. In fact, about a third of those involved were gay or
lesbian, mostly lesbian. One of them told the story of seeing an ad for this start-up church. She phoned the number
in the ad and mumbled, "Ah, what about, uh, alternative
lifestyles?" The man on the other end of the line boomed
back, "Oh, we're getting a lesbian minister." The deal was
done. Word spread in the well-networked lesbian community, and they checked it out. We particularly attracted
single and coupled lesbians with children. A few gay men
turned up as well.

Although JRUUC never was majority gay and lesbian by
any means, we did become identified in town as "the gay
church." Not that the label hurt us. Bisexuals felt comfortable identifying who they were. Plenty of straight people
came who recognized that, because we were welcoming
to LGBT people, we would welcome their whole selves.
The only people who felt excluded were those whose
homophobia made them uncomfortable in a place where
lesbian moms raised children together, where people of
the same sex might hold hands or share a quick kiss, and
where political activism around LGBT issues was a matter
of course.

When a local United Methodist church that was open
and affirming received threats, they reached out for com-

munity support. Our young church was one of the first places they turned to. With strong congregational support, I eagerly participated in a quickly crafted interfaith worship service. That first event led to an annual Coming Out Day service for the community that rotated among several supportive congregations. Most were Christian, one was Jewish, and then there were First Unitarian Society of Madison and us. I helped craft many of those services and later helped create a coalition of congregations called Coming Out, Coming Together.

I was part of a group of ministers who responded when Rev. Mel White of Soulforce came to Madison and challenged us to create a statement denouncing the misuse of Christian doctrine to condemn people based on sexual orientation. The primary point of contention in our initial discussion was whether the statement would be a Christian statement or a broader statement. As a Unitarian Universalist minister, I wanted my name, my participation, and my religious affiliation recognized. Our language needed to avoid the explicitly Christian and welcome all—or so I thought.

As I spoke with and listened to my colleagues, though, I realized that the problem for many LGBT people was not religion per se but rather that they had been condemned by Christian doctrine in Christian churches. In order to make the statement as strong as possible, it had to come from Christian mouths, from a Christian perspective. Otherwise, it might look as if people outside Christianity were condemning it. To address the need to include everyone, we created an option for non-Christians to sign on in support. I still worked on crafting the statement with my Christian colleagues and helped gather signatures and raise money for its publication. Later, when I was settled in Oklahoma City, I worked with another clergy group to use the Madison Affirmation as a model for our own statement about religion and acceptance without regard for sexual orientation.

Another transformative insight came to me while testifying before a state legislative committee against a law restricting marriage to heterosexual couples only. More than thirty JRUUC members, including many who were straight, rode a chartered bus or drove two and a half hours each way to attend the hearing. Several gave testimony, including a wise, articulate statement from ten-year-old Sol Kelly-Jones, daughter of two lesbians. A straight man from my congregation quoted scripture. I don't even remember what I said.

What sticks with me, though, was the testimony from the other side. Over and over, people quoted Leviticus and expounded on biblical values. Not one person who testified for the bill had an argument that was based outside religion, specifically Christian and Jewish religion. The creepiest moment of the day came when a man read the Leviticus text and expounded on the practice of stoning. A legislator on the panel asked in shock, "Are you saying that gay people should be killed?"

"I'm only telling you what God says in scripture," the man replied, his voice as hard as the stones he referred to. Clearly, he did believe that gay people should die. That moment has haunted and inspired my work on these issues ever since.

There were plenty of other opportunities for public witness: praying on the capitol steps, joining the religious community to participate in the gay pride parade, responses to Fred Phelps's picketing of gay-positive churches, and no doubt, moments I have long forgotten. The high profile on these issues, though, encouraged the development of the church and of another form of ministry that I would never have expected.

As the lesbian minister in town, I was asked regularly to conduct services of union, or weddings, for lesbian couples. It wasn't unusual for me to officiate two services in a weekend. As a result, I came to know a group of women I never would have met otherwise: working-class lesbians whose connection to the LGBT community was primarily through gay bars.

My encounter with these women challenged my expectations of what it meant to be a lesbian. They took on strongly stereotypical roles but never seemed to be playing at them. Butch and femme were no more "roles" than parent and child; they were simply who they were. They spoke in terms of marriage in the early nineties, when marriage equality was a distant dream.

I had been schooled in the feminist critique of marriage

and never saw it as part of my future, even though I have now been with the same partner for more than twenty-six years. The word *wife* sent shivers through my body, with its connotations of servitude and inequality. I believed then, as I do now, that one of the roles of LGBT people is to introduce new definitions of family, broader and more inclusive than the nuclear family. We would divide responsibilities in an unbiased, rather than a gender-specific, way. We would raise children without instilling in them the old ways of viewing gender. We would blaze the way, I thought, in introducing new ways of being in relationship—sexual and otherwise.

These folks, these women who met in bars and worked as mechanics and waitresses, seemed to want something I had nothing but disdain for: marriage that was conventional in every possible way, except the sex of those involved. They bought diamond engagement rings and referred to one another as "wife." I could not deny them the chance to pursue their heart's desire, even if that desire had been shaped according to societal conventions. In fact, I was much more willing to create a traditional-looking service for a lesbian couple than for a heterosexual one because simply doing such a ceremony challenged heterosexist, gender-biased doctrines.

Eventually, a woman from a couple I had joined in a holy union came to me, asking how to dissolve their marriage. Her wife had left her. Nothing legal could be done to ensure any rights, and there were no disagreements around property, but she wanted a divorce, a clear recognition that it was over, and that she had something to grieve. Together, we created a certificate of dissolution of their union. The ex even came in and signed it.

I also did pre- and postmarital counseling with more than one couple, though we never called it that. It all seemed like a ministry that needed to be done and that related to my call to the radically welcoming congregation I served. But there were at least two things that created barriers between this group of women and those who attended JRUUC: class and alcohol.

JRUUC had its share of working-class and even poor folks. Some of them were educated but poor. Others struggled with mental illness or physical disability that created obstacles. Some had been middle-class, but life had knocked them hard. To fit into the congregation, though, working-class and poor people at JRUUC needed to prize education, whether or not they had it, and to have some sort of aspiration for a different kind of life for themselves or their children. The working-class bar dykes I met tended not to share those values.

What's more, many of them bore the problem one expects in people whose lives are centered on bars—addiction. JRUUC also had its share of both recovering and active alcoholics and addicts. But many of the women I met from the gay bar culture were not interested in changing their lives. They could not see through the haze of alcohol or the indoctrination of society to understand the oppressions that shaped their lives. Most had little insight into how either of these things affected their relationships.

My lesbian minister identity gave me an open door to a place where I otherwise could not have walked. I was too educated, too middle class, too distant from their experiences. I struggled with how much to champion my own values on these issues and how much simply to walk with people where I could. I tended to lean toward the latter. Entering those lives taught me more about class and addiction than I had ever learned in seminary or workshops. I came to understand the destructiveness of internalized homophobia and how it can play out in addiction. I also learned about working-class perceptions of gender roles.

I left Madison to come to Oklahoma City, where I have family ties. It felt like stepping back in time, where attitudes towards LGBT people were not nearly as progressive. This time, though, I did not come as the identified lesbian minister. There already was one in town who had founded a United Church of Christ congregation with an outreach to the LGBT community. Relief. I was allowed to create a different niche where my sexuality defined me less.

Although I appreciated the experience the city of Madison gave me as its unofficial lesbian minister, the role came with a weight. Everything I said about justice for LGBT people could be more easily dismissed because of course I would say that—I was the lesbian minister. The identity made speaking out on other issues harder because I was perceived as being in a particular box. I didn't even realize how narrow my ministerial identity felt until I was freed of it.

Of course, I continue to work for LGBT equality but in a different way. My colleague Rev. Mark Christian is lead minister at First Unitarian Church of Tulsa; he's more out front on issues, including LGBT issues. What a luxury it is to have a heterosexual married man speak out for marriage equality, against hate crimes and bullying, and for nondiscrimination in employment and housing! Having allies, especially an ally who really gets it, makes a huge difference in my own energy for the work.

We meet weekly for coffee with an informal clergy support group that came together around issues of sexual orientation and gender identity. Our group includes ministers of welcoming churches, ministers who are themselves gay or lesbian, and ministers who are just plain open-minded.

Meeting regularly gives us the chance to respond to community issues as they arise and to put together community events that we hope will help the larger cause. For example, for several years, we did an annual Scripture and Homosexuality conference, to declare widely that the Bible, such a touchstone in this conservative evangelical place, does not condemn homosexuality in the way it is often claimed to. Later, the conference developed a broader focus, Sexuality and Spirituality.

And my role for a few years with Interweave Continental has helped me keep a foot in that lesbian minister identity. Serving as Interweave president while marriage equality became a more prominent issue for Unitarian Universalists led me into interesting reflection.

My ambivalence about marriage has not dissolved. I still wonder whether encouraging the pairing off of people, whatever their sexual orientation or gender, is the most productive way to ground society. Gay men, lesbians, bisexuals, transgender people, intersex people, and queer people all challenge traditional assumptions about gender and gender roles that need to be challenged. Sometimes, marriage seems like an assimilationist approach, where we earn our equality by wanting what everyone else wants.

So I have reluctantly supported marriage equality. It is true that everyone should have the same access to basic rights. However, I'd much rather those rights weren't accorded to marriage at all, that people could truly define their own family and economic units, without having to be tied to a specific monogamous sexual union. And I fear that the acquisition of marriage equality, which seems now to be inevitable, will mean a lost opportunity for creative examination of other ways we might organize ourselves into families. Rather, single people and different styles of families will continue to get the short end of the stick.

Last year, I heard a panel of youth of color in a plenary

session at Creating Change, the annual conference for activists sponsored by the National Gay and Lesbian Task Force. They cited studies they had done on the prevalence of homelessness among LGBTIQ youth, the frequency of hate crimes, and suicide. Why, wondered these articulate and prophetic young people, are we concerned about marriage, when people are literally dying? That's taking it up a notch.

I'm reminded that oppressions are complex. The youth of color who were speaking at Creating Change encountered discrimination and repression on at least three fronts—age, race, sexual orientation—and probably more. These and other very basic issues do not seem to be getting attention from our Unitarian Universalist congregations, much less from the broader culture. As my ministry continues to evolve, I am led to ask:

- How do we protect our LGBTIQ youth and young adults, physically and emotionally, in school and in the community?
- How do we protect our gay elders as they transition to places of even less control over their own lives than elderly heterosexuals have?
- How do we ensure nondiscrimination in housing and employment?
- How do we, as Unitarian Universalists, bring the gifts of our particular sexual orientations and gender identities to the larger world?
- How do we break the identification of religion

with persecution of those who do not fit hetero-sexist norms?

- How do we become conscious of our most basic assumptions about gender and sex? And how do we then make choices about whether or not to continue to accept those assumptions?

We're not all alike. We don't all want the same things, whether we're talking about LGBTIQ people or all humanity. Just as ministry has opened my eyes to worlds in which I had no direct experience, openness to the deepest dreams and desires of all people could be the key to eliminating oppression—if we are able to talk together fearlessly, if we are able to listen carefully.

May we have the strength and courage to do so.

◄o►

JONALU JOHNSTONE *has served as program minister of the First Unitarian Church, Oklahoma City, since 2002. From 2000 to 2002, as growth consultant for the Southwestern Unitarian Universalist Conference, she helped small and mid-size congregations understand and address their particular strengths and challenges. She also previously served the Channing Unitarian Universalist Church in Edmond as consulting minister; the James Reeb Unitarian Universalist Congregation in Madison, Wisconsin, as new congregation minister; and the Unitarian Universalist Association, working with the Dallas/Fort Worth Metropolitan Strategy for Growth. A graduate of Harvard Divinity School, Jonalu was ordained in 1993 by the Unitarian*

Universalist Fellowship of Greater Cumberland (Maryland), the lay-led congregation where she grew into leadership. She has contributed leadership to various community and Unitarian Universalist boards and committees, including Interweave Continental, the UU Ministers Association Committee on Ethics and Collegiality, the Southwestern Unitarian Universalist Conference, and the Oklahoma Food Co-op. She resides with her partner of more than twenty-five years, Jane Powell, a social worker and long-distance backpacker, in Oklahoma City.

TIME TO CHOOSE ANOTHER GAME

ANN SCHRANZ

Winters were cold in Waukesha, Wisconsin. Yet for most of my grade school years in the early- to mid-sixties, girls had to wear skirts or dresses during school hours. In a nod to practicality, however, we were allowed to wear long pants underneath our skirts while outdoors. This meant putting long pants on at home for the walk to school, taking them off at school, putting them on again for the walk home for lunch, taking them off upon returning to school after lunch, then putting the long pants on again for the walk home after school. Finally, at home, at last, it was the skirt that came off and the pants that stayed on. This clear example of socialization into traditional gender roles did not benefit girls.

The pressure was stepped up in middle school. In seventh grade, boys were assigned to take shop and girls were assigned to take home economics. One day in home ec, each girl was given a handful of clip-style wooden clothespins.

We were told to monitor each other's knees throughout the day in whatever classes we happened to have together. If any of us sat with our knees apart in any class, we were to give the unladylike offender a clothespin to clip onto her hem. She was supposed to go through the rest of the day with the clothespin clipped to her hem as a badge of shame. At the age when peer pressure was strongest, we were recruited to enforce traditional gender roles.

The days of enforcing ladylike behavior standards were still in the middle-school future, however, when I learned a valuable life skill. I learned to play dodgeball. Given the wardrobe changes needed for venturing into the great outdoors in the cold and snow, recess was held indoors in the gym. Dodgeball is a game in which players either try to hit other players with balls or try to avoid being hit. The way we played dodgeball, one team formed a circle and threw large rubber balls at members of the other team,

who milled around in the center of the circle.

My strategy allowed me to become one of the best players in my class. Most players in the middle of the circle scrambled frantically and clustered near each other. I stayed a short distance away from the agitated mass and moved slowly, not drawing attention to myself.

Gliding calmly instead of jumping around almost always resulted in my being among the last few surviving players inside the circle. I became very good at dodgeball defense.

I became very good at defense outside the gym as well. The trouble is that defense is not everything, not even in dodgeball, and dodgeball is not the only game in town. When the game is not the prerogative of the gym teacher, what shall we do with our precious time and energy? But when being emotionally guarded is no longer necessary, letting down one's guard can be tough. These are the reflections of a bisexual polyamorous Unitarian Universalist minister.

As background, I had moved to Florida in 1993 because I fell in love with a man I met in Nicaragua in 1990. Shortly after meeting him, I began identifying as bisexual. For ten years, I had identified as lesbian.

Coming out as bisexual was more difficult than coming out as lesbian, especially because it coincided with coming out as polyamorous. Polyamory is characterized by an openness to being in more than one concurrent sexually intimate relationship with the knowledge and consent of the other partners.

I was nervous about moving to a conservative part of the country, and I wondered how I could find politically and socially liberal friends. "Well, in Gainesville, they all go to the Unitarian Universalist Fellowship" was my friend's response. In 1993, I walked into my first Unitarian Universalist congregation and quickly became involved in committee and board leadership. I continued in leadership at the congregation in Tampa, where I had relocated to take a job.

I received support for the bisexual facet of my identity in both congregations. Support for the poly facet of my identity was muted. In 1999, as a layperson, I delivered a sermon called "Polyamory and Social Change" at the Unitarian Universalist Church of Tampa, apparently the second sermon on polyamory ever delivered from a Unitarian Universalist pulpit. I said, "About two years ago, I explored the possibility of becoming a Unitarian Universalist minister. In my research, everyone I talked to said that congregations were not ready to accept an openly polyamorous minister. My motivation for speaking to you today is to do my part so that in five years or twenty-five years, an otherwise qualified, openly polyamorous candidate might serve as minister in a Unitarian Universalist congregation."

The truth was that I wanted to serve as a Unitarian Universalist minister, and I did not want to wait twenty-five years to do it. I felt both pushed and pulled into ministry. A less than satisfying job pushed me. A longstanding interest in how we make meaning in our lives pulled me into ministry. So after seven years as a lay leader in two congregations, I applied to Starr King School for the Ministry and was accepted. Naively, I thought that getting in and out of seminary would be the most difficult part of the journey to ministry. In fact, the ministerial credentialing process was far more difficult.

Ministerial credentialing involves documenting relevant education and experience over a number of years. It also involves interviewing with two groups of powerful people: the Regional Subcommittee on Candidacy (RSC) and the Ministerial Fellowship Committee (MFC). Those interviews have a high-stakes feel because the work of these groups is to give a stamp of unqualified approval, a stamp of qualified approval, or a stamp of disapproval. The interviewers' comments and questions reflect Unitarian Universalist norms and hopes. The interviews are a snapshot of our movement's dynamics at a particular time.

At the interview with the RSC, I was asked to talk about my committed relationship with a woman partner. The relationship had become a long-distance one when I moved to California to begin seminary classes. I talked about it, then volunteered that I had a male partner as well. I debated whether to mention him since we were not in a committed relationship and did not live together. However, remaining silent would have felt like an error of omission. I had to be the change I wanted to see in the world. I wanted a world in which relationship health mattered, not relationship form, so I risked being open and honest.

What happened next startled me. A committee member became agitated and told me that I could not call myself committed to the woman partner if I was not monogamous with her. I could say that I was "dating," he continued, but I could not say that ours was a committed relationship. I was stunned. I was prepared for their curiosity and even for their hostility, but I was not prepared to be told how to describe my own relationship. Before seeing me again, the committee asked me to see a counselor, to moderate my enthusiasm for a particular philosopher, and to talk with ministers about polyamory and ministry. I was encouraged to contact some of the first out gay or lesbian ministers, in particular, since their experiences might be comparable to my own.

"If you can't stand the heat, stay out of the kitchen. Oh, and by the way, you have no idea how hot it is in the kitchen!" That is how I interpreted the feedback. Although disappointed, I wanted to use the conversations with the ministers to raise their consciousness about polyamory and not just to raise my consciousness about ministry. Rather than contact a few ministers, I contacted a dozen of them, and I took careful notes during our phone conversations. Acutely aware of the power differential between us, I called upon my dodgeball skills in these conversations: no sudden verbal moves and a lot of calm gliding.

Although I did not at the time have the language to put it this way, I did my best to create sacred space into which their thoughts and feelings could be released. Some of their comments seemed to be based on fear. Some seemed to be steering me away from parish ministry into community ministry, advising me that the problem was not so much the credentialing process as it was the level of anxiety in congregations. You run the risk of never being called, several ministers warned.

Hearing such comments from ministers who had probably heard similar remarks when they were doing the hard work of breaking a path into ministry for gays and lesbians was disconcerting. Some comments sounded remarkably antifeminist, sex-negative, and overly simplistic regarding the variety of ways that adults handle close relationships. My prior experience had been that Unitarian Universalism supported a more progressive family structure than the kind shown on fifties television. Yet some ministers strongly implied that congregations were that conservative.

It was easy to do the dodgeball glide, sidestepping inflammatory statements. The most irritating comments, the ones built on flimsy, inaccurate assumptions, came from ministers who were clearly in pain. They still felt pain at having been misunderstood years before, as they were blazing a trail. You will be misunderstood, I heard. To be misunderstood is to be scarred, I gathered, even for the well-adjusted and the successful.

There were some bright spots: those ministers whose kindness and caring warmed my heart, affirmed me, and bolstered my spirit. For example, one straight minister said, "People tend to be parochial, thinking that our way is the best way. Relationships are demanding. I don't know how one maintains more than one. Polyamory brings sexuality up front. This is difficult for a minister. People notice how you dress, move, touch, where your sensitive areas are. We're really not very sophisticated. We are very amateur. There is so much energy around sexuality because we're not able to be more adept. We are repressive."

She continued, "Take your spiritual life seriously. Make your practice central. This will help you through the troubled times. Ministry is a calling that asks everything of you. Take on one or two battles. What does the world most need? This is most serious work. What does the world ask of you? This is not about success. All of the world's great religious leaders were failures at the time. It's a strange world, the realm of love. We're nervous at the power of it.

"Your challenge is to distinguish your path from that of illicit betrayal, cheating, and affairs," she concluded. "Try to help people understand that polyamory is different from lies and confusion. Clarify what you're about, how it's safe, sane, and holy, how it's not about getting into a mess. People are very, very wounded. The hurt and anger around betrayal is ferocious. This work is doable and needs to be done. Conversations often veer back to sexuality because that is where the energy lies. This may be something to devote your life to. I applaud you. It will take time. Listen to where God is telling you to go." Although the "God language" did not quite resonate, I feel drawn, as a mystic and humanist, to continue doing my part to shape a Unitarian Universalism relevant for contemporary lives.

In retrospect, how might the process have been different? The RSC might have taken a more balanced approach. For example, the Committee might have asked me to talk with ministers about not only a topic they expected to be disheartening but also about one they expected to be heartening. "Talk with some of our pioneering lesbian or gay ministers about their experiences," they might have said. "Oh, and while you are talking with them, ask them about what they find fulfilling about ministry." Our lives are made up of disheartening and heartening experiences. The credentialing process could do a better job of encouraging candidates to develop a habit of eliciting both. A creative life is not primarily about defensive moves.

As I recall, MSC members asked me over a dozen questions about polyamory at my interview. I felt almost cheated by not having the chance to answer very many questions about a wider variety of ministerial topics. The MFC feedback? I should attend an antiracism workshop, and I should talk with a public relations professional about how best to respond to possible media inquiries about polyamory. Ironically, I believe I responded to their questions using basic public relations principles: Stick to your message regardless of the question, and don't lose control of your emotions. It occurred to me later that the MFC may have considered me too emotionally controlled. I may have reached the limits of dodging.

I am in my sixth year as minister, and same-sex marriage has been a hot topic in California for the entire time. I am in my fourth year as a settled minister, after serving a different congregation as its intentional interim minister for two years. I was out as bi and poly while in the search process, which says a lot about Unitarian Universalists. During my ministerial internship, I had asked my internship committee for guidance on how to describe myself in the search packet. "Don't use the p word," they advised. "Say that you are in a committed relationship and that the relationship is open." To the credit of the Unitarian Universalist Association's Transitions Office, they made sure that each congregation seriously considering calling me saw the p word in a write-up about me.

As it happens, my being out as bi and poly has not caused distress in the congregation, knock on wood. My philosophical reservations about marriage, on the other hand, were among the reasons cited by a lesbian couple who recently left the congregation. Experiences such as the grade-school and middle-school gender role socialization primed me to be responsive to feminist consciousness-raising in college. I learned then that marriage began as a form of property management, with women as the

property. Even regarding the companionate marriage model held up today, I am not a fan of marriage. Yes, I officiate at marriages of congregants. No, I do not think that marriage—same-sex or otherwise—is a fair basis upon which to distribute social benefits.

That is why I was pleased to be recruited onto the board of directors of the Alternatives to Marriage Project (www.unmarried.org). I volunteer on my own time, not as part of my work in the congregation. Just as Unitarian Universalists are wise to have a handy elevator speech about their faith handy, I have had to come up with my own about the work of the project: "Single and poly people are people too. Marriage should not be the gold standard for evaluating loving, healthy adult relationships. "

In relation to LGBTQ issues and identity, I wish the Unitarian Universalist Association (UUA) would stop regarding marriage equality as something inherently and uniformly desired by LGBTQ people. The UUA's promotion of same-sex marriage has diverted dollars and energy into supporting a fundamentally flawed institution. I am proud to be among the early signers of the Beyond Same-Sex Marriage statement by queer activists and allies (www .beyondmarriage.org).

In supporting the Alternatives to Marriage Project, I am leaving dodgeball behind. I am not sure what this new game is called, but I know that it's fun. It's collaborative. It's the next level of a team sport for me. It's risky. My heart ached when the lesbian couple said they were leaving in part to find a Unitarian Universalist congregation whose minister was more enthusiastic about marriage. However, I have learned that heartache comes with the territory when the territory is ministry. Laypeople and clergy alike are engaged in ministries. Thankfully, the territory also comes with fulfillment.

Readers, some of you may be wondering whether Unitarian Universalism is ready for someone like you. I conclude by relaying these words by seminary president Rev. Dr. Rebecca Parker. She encouraged me at a time in the credentialing process when I needed it. Do not just focus on what you are being asked to do, she said. Stay grounded in what you are asking of them: to appreciate your gifts. Use the experience of encountering prejudice as a way to empathize with others who encounter prejudice. Yes, Unitarian Universalism is ready for a minister like you. May it be so!

◄o►

ANN SCHRANZ *is a graduate of Starr King School for the Ministry in Berkeley, California. She has a degree in journalism from the University of Wisconsin-Madison and an MBA from Pepperdine University. Ann was ordained in 2005 at Orange Coast Unitarian Universalist Church in Costa Mesa, California. Remaining in California, she began serving as the settled minister at Monte Vista Unitarian Universalist Congregation in Montclair in 2007, after serving as the interim minister at the Unitarian Universalist Fellowship of Santa Cruz County for two years. Ann is a member of Unitarian Universalists for Polyamory Awareness (www.uupa.org), and she is on the board of directors of the Alternatives to Marriage Project (www.unmarried.org).*

THEN I FEEL SEEN

DREW JOHNSTON

At an annual Pride Day party in our town, our congregation had a table that was well staffed by volunteers, and we passed out dozens of cards with this message from me:

> I used to think that my sexual orientation and gender identity would keep me away from religion. So many great things are possible in a community where you are truly welcomed. I found a religion that welcomes me as a complete person—more than tolerating or accepting—welcoming in wholeness. Unitarian Universalists say that everyone has value, that everyone should be treated well, that what we do matters more than creeds and dogma.
>
> Here's the cool thing—they don't just say it, they act that way, too! I should know, I am a queer bi/trans Unitarian Universalist, and the Senior Minister here.

See you in church?
—Drew

I so much wanted to believe that it was true, especially the "cool thing" part of it. It was partially true, of course, but my experience has not been entirely positive.

I have been internally marginalized, oppressing myself as I attempted to live a normal happy life while facing the disconnect between who I felt myself to be and who I showed myself to be. I was externally marginalized because I never quite fit others' expectations. Coming out at work and enjoying the support of several people was, in some ways, the epitome of joy, the moment in which I was most whole as a minister and most optimistic about my calling to ministry within the Unitarian Universalist Association. The lifetime of incongruity between my internal sense of identity and my public presentation could be left in the

past. I could now serve a congregation with clarity and confidence that I was being my complete self.

Being Unitarian Universalist did not make me optimistic, but at times it has supported my inherent optimism. Twenty years before I sent that message, I found this place, this religious enterprise where, finally, I did not have to conform to a set of expectations like those that had always excluded me from other institutions. Anyone who met me at the time I first came to a Unitarian Universalist congregation could have easily assumed I was a typical thirty-something, heterosexual male, married, and with a child. I never claimed to be straight, and no one ever asked. Within the intimate conversations that spouses have, my wife knew about my past and my certain feeling that I was bisexual, or at least not heterosexual, and we placed a high value on monogamous commitment. We seemed to have it worked out, and I felt blessed to be in that marriage. We were so compatible that I felt no pressure to take any action other than savoring our time together and being faithfully committed.

Soon after getting involved in my first Unitarian Universalist congregation, I became involved in political action against an antigay initiative that was on the state ballot. For the most part, I think I was seen as a straight ally to those whose rights were being threatened by the proposed initiative. Since I was leading the statewide Unitarian Universalist effort, I attended many rallies and public events during that campaign season, and frequently spoke to the press as a representative of Unitarian Universalism. That was, essentially, my job. Several remarkable things happened during those months.

For one thing, I was impressed to meet Unitarian Universalists from across the state and surrounding states who were eager and willing to make some effort to protect the rights of LGBTQ people. I was also impressed by what was happening inside of me. I had found something of great value in my small congregation, a place where I could be myself. The years since then have been both the best of times and the worst.

We defeated that antigay initiative. During the process, I was frequently encouraged to consider entering the ministry. The more I considered that possibility, the more interested I became—and the more terrified I felt. If the act of finding a congregation and a religious institution that did not automatically exclude me had been liberating, what else might change if I deepened my commitment to this religious movement by devoting my life to ministry?

I had a sense I was risking everything: my security, my family, my carefully constructed identity. During the ensuing years, I lost them all. Something has replaced them, or at least serves as a placeholder, but finding religion has come at a cost.

Politics has never been my strong suit, but during the political campaign year, I traveled the state and talked to people about oppression. I was struck by the passion of so many Unitarian Universalists who had the comfortable status of being in the majority; when other people's rights were at risk, they would rise to the occasion and fight for equality. I was smitten.

Within a couple of years, my family and I left our congregation so I could attend Starr King School for the Ministry in Berkeley, California. At school, I never claimed to be straight, but I admit I was presumed straight. Many people at the school wanted to categorize me in ways I had not experienced elsewhere. Because I was well-married and parenting with my spouse, some wanted me to be a "normal," straight person. Some even held us up as an example of a family that remained intact through the challenges of seminary. A few who listened more attentively to me understood that I was a monogamous bisexual or pansexual person, not quite the same as a straight person. An interesting aspect of seminary is that being straight and married does not convey the same degree of privilege as it does in society at large. In some small way, being presumed straight is not helpful, but I never pressed the issue.

While serving my first congregation, I worked hard to convey that I knew full well the reality of being bisexual, as well as the reality of being a faithful monogamous partner. Eventually, some people seemed to recognize the value in dismantling the categories into which we put people. At the same time, other people began to murmur.

A member of the congregation once said to another in my presence, "Okay, I get it, the minister is bisexual. But bisexuals are promiscuous; they have to be. So Drew is promiscuous." As disturbing as it was that this person would make such an assertion at all, it was even more disturbing that they did so in my presence, as if I were not there. I began to realize that the religious institution I felt could hold me was also the place in which I felt marginalized in ways that had never occurred elsewhere. "Imagine that," I thought. "I have become invisible."

I left that congregation without my family, the hardest move of my life. I was aware that certain members of the congregation would make up stories about why I left, stories that would involve their ideas of promiscuous bisexuals and infidelity. The discomfort of knowing that people were making up stories, though, paled in comparison to the pain of losing my family.

A small, saving distraction arrived in the form of my next congregation.

This congregation seemed delighted to welcome a bisexual minister! I recall my visit as a candidate, when I was spending time with various groups in the congregation. The president pulled me aside and said with some excitement, "I get it now! You're not gay, you're bisexual. You actually loved your wife; your marriage didn't end because you were gay!" I know this was supposed to be a show of support and understanding; I tried to take it as it was meant rather than how it felt. It felt, however, like I was becoming less and less visible to the people I was committed to serve.

As is so often the case, this congregation was full of lovely and generous Unitarian Universalists. I was touched by the interest they took in my personal life; they seemed genuinely pleased when I was dating, and they welcomed the man I was dating with enthusiasm. Although I had a nagging sense that something was awry, they invited me to stay after my second year and voted to affirm that invitation. I accepted their call but was never installed as their settled minister.

Issues related to being queer could not have been the source of my foreboding, because the congregation knew I was bisexual, seemed to enjoy seeing me dating, and seemed to care about my happiness. Like many of our congregations, this one was somewhat isolated, and they were concerned about my ability to find a steady social life. I shared that concern, but as I've said, I am inherently optimistic.

The nagging sense of foreboding that I felt was, in fact, justified. I think what unfolded speaks to the expectations we have of our clergy as much as it speaks to the choices I made and the identity I had not yet claimed.

I had found a social life of sorts, not far away, but far enough not to create an image problem. I dated a few men and, although dating men was fun, I did not feel that gay male expectations of communication were any more of a fit than straight male expectations. Nothing lasting came out of dating, but I developed strong friendships with colleagues in the area and believed I was content.

Things happen, though, in reaction to internal fears mixed with a commitment to serve, combined with a strong dose of loneliness. On the surface, I was addressing questions of equal access to marriage for LGBTQ people; the "Don't Ask, Don't Tell" (DADT) policy of the U.S. military, which, for seventeen years, prohibited openly gay men or lesbians from serving; the congregation's assumptions about how I should be living; and the one major internal identity issue I was hoping to ignore the rest of my life.

Because I thought I would never have another serious relationship and because of my strong feeling that DADT was unjust, I married a close lesbian friend who was in the military. I wanted to challenge DADT and to be supportive of my friend in our marginalized status. Given the history of marriage in America, it seemed reasonable to get married to provide each of us a sense of security and support. I combined my activist motive for subverting DADT with my personal motive to be less alone.

After the fact, I realized that I had no idea how to explain my marriage to the congregation in a way that made sense. I probably waited too long to tell the congregation about this marriage, and my attempt to keep it in context failed.

The reasons relationships between a minister and congregation unravel are sometimes difficult to determine. In the wake of a great deal of success, turbulence is often brewing. Because I could not, in practice, have a complete life while living in the neighborhood of the church, I spent a great deal of time forty minutes away. I could not fully explain that I got married because the most serious relationship I could muster up was with a friendly lesbian serving our country.

The bookend on my experience was captured in a new congregational statement that effectively said, "We liked having a gay minister, and since you got married, you're not gay enough." In the way the congregation saw me and talked about me, I had ceased being bisexual once they saw me dating men; until I married, they had recast me as gay. As one of my professors commented upon hearing this story, "Well, there are a lot of ways to get in trouble."

Underlying all of this was my still unclaimed gender identity. I did a great deal of soul-searching after my difficult departure from the congregation. I certainly immersed myself in every opportunity I could to answer the following questions: How did I contribute to this event? Is ministry a place I can stay?

After leaving my second congregation, I took the opportunity for a mid-career assessment at one of the Boston-area centers for ministry used by Unitarian Universalists. One of those best of / worst of moments occurred at the center. On the second day, my counselor said quite plainly, "Until you address your gender identity issues, you are not going to be happy or successful in ministry." I had not been expecting this! I was not attempting to deal with gender identity issues; in fact, I hoped that this most challenging aspect of my being could just wait until I was . . . was what? I just didn't want to deal with it.

My wise counselor knew I had to address this aspect of myself. She seemed to know that I was prepared to listen. Indeed, my response was one of recognition and chagrined acceptance. I returned to the West Coast filled with hope and trepidation that I might be able to remain in ministry and discover my true being all at the same time. I spent time with a gender identity specialist and accepted a short-term ministry in the Midwest once I knew there were gender specialists there. For the third time in my career, I entered a congregation as a non-straight, non-male/non-female.

Since seminary, I had spoken of myself as "born male, but with a significant female aspect." At the same time, I would claim to be "neither gay nor straight." So it was in my early days of what was supposed to be a six-month interim ministry. As in other congregations I had served, things went very well for a while. We did an unusual thing and converted the interim position into a full-time consulting ministry. I served for three and a half years. Most of my tenure there was challenging but successful—until I claimed my transgender identity.

I had spent several years exploring and affirming my identity and had been taking female hormones for almost two years. For the first time in my adult life, I felt an increasing congruity between my inner way of being and my body. This was not a matter of appearance but of chemistry, I guess. I felt like I did not have to constantly interpret my thoughts through a filter to make them come out as "male." I felt like I was getting access to my original way of being and could let go of the years of struggle to fit into a male role in life.

I was in a serious relationship with a woman when I started the process of transitioning from male to female, but we went our separate ways soon after I began. We knew that adjusting to the changes would be difficult, which was one reason we could not stay close at that time. We did return to a very close relationship later, but transition took its toll. She was well-known at church, and folks were concerned about whether we were both doing okay after we broke up. I think their concern also distracted them from the changes I was experiencing.

My appearance was never my primary motive for transitioning, but it did start to change. During this period, I became involved with another woman, and I suppose that helped deflect questions about what was happening to my appearance and behavior.

The wise career counselor I had seen in Boston had helped me devise a coming-out strategy that I was partly successful in implementing. One key piece of the strategy that failed was to arrange some form of visible denominational support, some way of showing that the Unitarian Universalist Association approved, if not endorsed, the existence of a male-to-female transgender minister in one of our congregations. I did not succeed in arranging anything I could point to that said, "Not only am I a Unitarian Universalist minister and a male-to-female transgender individual, I am also supported by my denomination."

However, the announcement that I was transgender made much more sense than the announcement of my marriage a few years before.

My optimism always returns eventually; at least it has thus far. Although I had to take a significant pay cut and move far across the country in order to serve as a one-year interim minister, I am enjoying a significantly more positive experience now. There is a little energy from the congregation indicating that they don't want to talk about the reality of having a trans minister. In fact, I've only been asked one question about it so far, and the question itself helped me feel visible. After a lovely potluck dinner to welcome me, I spoke for a while about my thoughts on coming to the congregation and what I hoped we would do together in the transitional time. I mentioned that we didn't have to talk about my gender status, but it would seem a little weird if we didn't. Then I took questions.

The first question was about gendered pronouns: Did I prefer male or female? This brought up some interesting thoughts. As a transgender person, I have experienced the opposite of being welcomed every day. People notice something that doesn't fit their notion of what they should be seeing. For the most part, I either get stared at or ignored. I was thinking about these experiences before I answered the question.

As I began talking, I did not know where I was going to end up. I explained how my position on the question of gendered pronouns had evolved. Then I heard myself finally answer the question. I said that I like it when people at least alternate. I said, "Then I feel seen." That struck a deep chord within me: I feel seen. The act of asking the question helped me feel seen too. Just today, my president embarrassed me slightly by telling the congregation that I had just had a birthday. In the course of the announcement, he used feminine pronouns to refer to me. They sang to me, and I felt seen, and loved.

My experience of being queer and a Unitarian Universalist has covered much of the LGBTQ spectrum. I have at times been invisible or, at least, less than fully visible. For a while, much of that invisibility was by my own design. Having found a religious home, I did not want to lose it due to rejection of my way of being. I spent most of my life rejecting myself, so I speak with some authority on this matter.

In my more visible moments, I have stood as an ally to those who had more at risk than I did. I have taken the risk of naming myself and claiming my identity. Recently, I have simply gone about my work being who I am. I feel seen when I am asked how I want to be seen.

There is one other moment I will treasure always. My coming-out Sunday happened to coincide with the birthday celebration for a delightful eighty-something member of the congregation. I went to sit with her during the social hour and wish her a happy birthday. Having just listened to my coming-out sermon, she had something to tell me. As I was beginning to speak, she

interrupted, took my hand, and said, "I'm sorry it's been so hard for you."

It is hard, and I don't know if I can keep doing it. I understand change, I thrive on transformation, and these are qualities I bring to my ministry. I know that it is a lot to hope for a congregation that can continue to embrace a minister who changes while serving them. Some people like to joke about my steps from married and presumed straight, to bisexual, to gay, to married again, back to single, bisexual, and transgender.

I am now single and queer. The most important relationship in my life is parenting my son, now a young adult. I don't know how much more change I might experience; I've noticed such things are hard to predict. I've devoted a significant portion of my life to Unitarian Universalism. In some ways, it has been a blessing I didn't know I needed.

The first time I spoke in my home congregation as a layperson, I quoted Anna Louise Strong, who wrote, "To fall in love is easy, even to remain in it is not difficult; our human loneliness is cause enough. But it is a hard quest worth making to find a comrade in whose steady presence one steadily becomes the person one desires to be." I did not specifically desire this outcome; that was my lack of foresight. I am, however, steadily becoming the person I need to be, the person I am. Unitarian Universalism has been, if not a steady presence, at least a frequent companion with me in this hard journey. As long as there are moments when someone is open enough to ask how I care to be addressed, and moments when a kind woman will interrupt her own celebration to reach out and take my hand, then there is hope for this relationship to continue.

I can't spend the rest of my career moving every year or two into a new interim minister position; something else will have to happen. Meanwhile, I have met Unitarian Universalists all over the country. In my best moments, I remain smitten by the folks who make the effort to better ourselves and our world.

See you in church?

—◦—

DREW JOHNSTON *was born in Boise, Idaho, and graduated from Starr King School for the Ministry in 1999. Although often drawn to the western United States, Drew ends up in decidedly non-western places, serving congregations in transitional times. This work reaffirms that change is a constant, and often desirable, aspect of life. Some changes are less expected, and addressing gender identity was such an example for Drew. In the ongoing search for wholeness, Drew has faith that authenticity is worth the messiness of claiming a genuine identity. Ministry follows several careers, ranging from musical instrument builder to school administrator to carpenter. A recurrent theme for Drew is one of relational teaching and learning encounters. Ministry seems to be an endless field of opportunity to learn and teach, second only to family and personal relationships.*

THE SPIRITUALITY OF DISCOMFORT

SHARON GROVES

God is unity but always works in variety.
—Ralph Waldo Emerson

I was raised on the secular side of Unitarianism. Good works, intellectual curiosity, principled living—these were our guideposts, and empirical evidence was as close as we got to the Divine. About five years ago, I started working at a lesbian, gay, bisexual, transgender advocacy organization, the Human Rights Campaign (HRC), in their newly formed Religion and Faith Program. Advocacy work on behalf of LGBTQ people fit my good works model—but religious advocacy was something else altogether.

Prior to working at HRC, I wandered in the wilderness of vocation. Trained to be an English professor and working for a feminist interdisciplinary journal, I felt something was missing. Like many, I started going to church after the World Trade Center attacks on September 11, 2001. I landed at All Souls Church Unitarian in Washington, D.C., and there I discovered grace. I would never have called it grace at the time; I was deeply suspicious of all religious concepts. Yet grace showed up all the same: in the combination of sadness and hope that defined that brief moment before President Bush started the war in Iraq; in the longing I shared with people searching for community with those they did not know; and in our countercultural practice of seeking to be with each other in ways that did not reduce us all to commodities bartered in a marketplace called networking. At All Souls, I felt valued not for the things I had done but for my humanity. I discovered a deep peace and have never looked back.

All Souls was also the source for my deepening activism. I realized fairly quickly that a church context offered untapped resources for activism. Simply by enrolling a few people in the idea of a panel presentation, a discussion group, or a rally, I could be assured a space, equipment, and an audience. You could make things happen in church. All Souls became my epicenter; everything I did circled out from the spiritual growth, justice work, and church leadership I engaged in there.

When I began working at HRC in 2005, my religious neighborhood changed, and I found myself forced to change with it in ways that were deeply uncomfortable. I had embraced religious-based activism within a lay Unitarian Universalist context, but I was unprepared for how my spiritual sense of self would be challenged by people from other faiths who also felt called to activist work on behalf of the LGBTQ community.

I had to wrestle with my distrust of other religious expressions, particularly Christianity. Before working at HRC, I experienced Christianity as the faith of aliens. Despite the fact that my partner's family is Episcopalian and my sister-in-law and her husband are Episcopalian priests, Christianity felt like a mysterious, foreboding club filled with rituals available only to the initiated. I was threatened by its mysterious force. As with many people who feel threatened, I made snap judgments. In my mind, Christianity was a religion of intolerance, and the deeper the believer, the more conservative and intolerant the believer.

Lurking behind my arrogance was fear. How do you talk to people who don't hold rational argument as foundational? How do you establish your footing? I thought the best way to deal with religious people, particularly Christians, was to keep my distance. To encounter Christianity from a place of respect and welcome threatened my rational faith grounding. It was like standing in quicksand.

I soon began to realize, however, that holding my ground was actually what was keeping me stuck. My intolerance of Christianity was the real quicksand that was swallowing up my spiritual life. If I was going to be effective at my job, I had to reexamine lingering preconceptions, and in doing so, I also had to open myself up to the discomfort of a spiritual journey. I had to take a leap of faith.

My intolerance of Christianity quickly morphed into

anxious inadequacy. I was apologetic for my Unitarian Universalist faith, which seemed murky compared to those traditions that offered seemingly smooth and confident access to the sacred language of God and scripture. People from the more traditional religions seemed to have it easier. God, salvation, the afterlife were concepts that seemed to float effortlessly off the tongues of others. My tongue yearned for this ease with sacred language, but my spirit struggled. What would it mean to be inauthentic in the expression of faith? The right to authentic expression of belief is after all a hard-won Unitarian Universalist principle. To falsely claim a religious space that is not ours comes close to sacrilege in our world. Our faith, after all, evolves from people who challenged the status quo of their time and took as sacred the individual's spiritual journey. But I didn't want the journey; I wanted certainty and the eloquence that comes with it. I wanted God, and I didn't know if I could find it

as a Unitarian Universalist.

I've discovered that it's not the differences but the similarities among people of faith that are often the most unsettling. Recognizing similarities has a way of shattering the dichotomies that define our religious traditions. Just as Jesus speaks to us through his ministry to the outcast, I have seen LGBT outsiders, people who have been marginalized or denied a place in their religious homes of origin, re-imagine the church in ways that make it unrecognizable to itself. When the rules of religious doctrine become less important than the healing message of God's love, faith begins to transcend even the most entrenched ideologies. Feeling truly welcome and loved is one of the most powerful experiences I've encountered in the religious practices of others.

This recognition is, however, unsettling. I've come to realize that the spiritual journey is not a beautiful winding road among picturesque ancient ruins. It's not a summer holiday in Umbria. The spiritual journey, or mine at any rate, is rarely peaceful, picturesque, or romantic. For me, it has consisted of a lot of embarrassing encounters with my own biases, limitations, and insecurities. But when I can get out of my own way, what I find is grace.

Through my work at HRC, I've witnessed extraordinary grace and power in the faiths of others. I've been part of a fall-out-of-your-seat, speaking-in-tongues Pentecostal service that nearly led me to full-immersion baptism; I've gone to Seder celebrations that so beautifully invoked food, community, and ritual as a meditation on freedom that I seriously entertained Jewish conversion. I've talked at length to Southern Baptists, Orthodox Jews, Sunni Muslims, Roman Catholics, among others, and with such conversations, I find myself reborn in the faith of the other.

Rev. Robert Hardies speaks about the experience of being born again as a work in progress: "We are born again and again and again." This has been my experience encountering other faiths. I have been deepened and transformed as a religious person, but I'm sometimes left feeling as if I have no place to call home.

I recently attended the funeral service for the father of a remarkable man, Rev. Dennis Wiley. Rev. Wiley and his wife, Rev. Christine Wiley, are copastors of Covenant Baptist United Church of Christ congregation and members of HRC's Religion Council. They have been extraordinary advocates for issues facing the citizens of Washington, D.C., from housing rights to economic empowerment. I came to know them, however, through their work for LGBT equality. They are heroes in the LGBTQ world for their brave stance.

Dennis Wiley lost his mother and father less than two weeks apart and presented the eulogy for both. In his father's eulogy, Dennis shared that he had thought about his parents' inevitable death for a long time. He was close to both and wasn't at all certain he would be able to sit in the front row during their funeral, let alone give the eulogy. But there he was. Rev. Wiley not only found the inner strength to eulogize his mother and father's passing but he also gave one of the most generous sermons I've heard. He took the opportunity to fortify his congregation in their belief in God. "God gave my father the strength to not fall into a depression. God gave me the strength to speak in front of you, and God will give you the strength when you need it most." Lean on God, he told us. Know that death is not the end, but something much more glorious is on its way.

I witnessed the power of Rev. Wiley's faith at that service, I saw its effect on his congregation, and I felt it in my own body. I was transformed by his sermon. I became a believer.

I didn't stay there. I struggle with the idea of an afterlife, and I sure can't describe it in the ways I've heard others do. But gone is my arrogance, my mere tolerance of others' faith, and in its place is a desire to embrace inspiration when it comes my way, to let it work on me and to share what I'm witnessing.

Finding ways to speak about these experiences in a Unitarian Universalist context is a challenge. We love to talk about interfaith dialogue, but I've rarely seen us allow others' faiths to shake our foundations. Yet our history is not just about being liberal in a sea of conservative traditions, it's about seeking deep transformation at the core of our beings. Ours is a faith of discomfort.

Uncomfortable with the Christian Trinity, early Unitarians imagined a new theology based on the power of unity. Uncomfortable with the prevailing concept of hell, early Universalists imagined a new kind of heaven based on universal salvation. Uncomfortable with our history, Unitarian Universalists still carry the tensions of a Christian past and a multifaith present. This discomfort is expressed in the way we talk about ourselves outside our congregations. For some of us, just saying "I go to church" is embarrassing. Stating that we go to a Unitarian Universalist congregation, what many see as the antichurch church, embarrasses others.

We're uncomfortable when we're together, which is perhaps why we feel the need to proclaim over and over again who we are and what we believe—or rather who we are not and what we don't believe. Like it or not, we are continually discovering, reinventing, and proclaiming our faith. If the weakness of our faith is that we are forever reinventing ourselves based on our contact with others, it is also our most sacred treasure. As our forebear Ralph Waldo Emerson stated, "Our strength grows out of our weakness. Whilst a man sits on the cushion of advantages, he goes to sleep. When he is pushed, tormented, defeated, he has a chance to learn something." If we can allow it, we can be transformed through encounters with "the other." We have much to offer the religious and secular world.

Dr. Eboo Patel, a Muslim writer and interfaith activist, speaks frequently about a seldom-emphasized aspect of Dr. Martin Luther King's legacy. As a young student at Morehouse College, King attended a lecture by the renowned preacher, intellectual, and activist Mordecai Johnson. Johnson told the audience that the best model for civil rights work was found in Mahatma Gandhi's witness. Patel speculates that, in response, King asked himself, "What is it in my faith that connects with that great love in Gandhi's faith?" King, the son and grandson of Baptist ministers, was strengthened, not compromised, by his encounter with Gandhi. He came back from India invoking the Divine that speaks across traditions, never losing sight of his ministry's grounding in the Black church and the teachings of Jesus Christ.

King and Gandhi didn't simply have a nice exchange about different beliefs. Their encounter was transformative, an urgent cry for human connection in the crucible of struggle. Principled passive resistance to unequal treatment rather than aggression became the way the civil rights movement brought attention to the devastating consequences of racism.

Those who work on justice issues know that Unitarian Universalism's core values are critical in the struggle for justice. What we contemplate less often are the particular gifts we have to offer in interfaith encounters. Ours is a faith that places its emphasis on the journey over the destination. We are a faith that understands discomfort with belief. Our faith celebrates difficult encounters. We know how to serve as a bridge between the secular and the religious, as well as among intrareligious worlds. Unitarian Universalists demand an authentic clearing and revitalization of all religious concepts: God, the Divine, the soul, the sacred, grace. Each must be felt and experienced anew— personally, in exchanges between individuals, and within our congregations.

The paradox of the Unitarian Universalist journey is that we cannot fully and openly encounter the faiths of others if we are not simultaneously deepening our own faith. If we emphasize the interfaith at the cost of our self-discovery, we cannot be effective interfaith partners.

As we encounter other religions, we need to return to the question, what core Unitarian Universalism belief gives meaning to our lives? My core belief is that a Divine spark exists in all of us. This principle challenges me at my core. Can I really see the Divine in the homeless people I too easily pass on the street? Can I hold in my heart the lives of people dying around the globe, even though I will never meet them and their numbers are mind-boggling? Can I see the Divine spark in those who systematically try to tear down the work for LGBTQ justice that occupies me day in and day out? It can be hard, exhausting work. Yet when I rest in the spark of the Divine in me and in those around me, I find a freedom and purpose to my life not found elsewhere.

We Unitarian Universalists have been extraordinary leaders in the work for LGBTQ justice. The Religion and Faith Program at HRC turns to Unitarian Universalists first and most often when are looking to do work within congregations around the country. Student groups, PFLAG, and other secular organizations turn first to our congregations when they need a space to meet. We offer sanctuary for people who have been bruised by their faiths, people who can't find a home that works for them in another's faith, or people who are unchurched.

What we have not been as of yet is true *faith* leaders in our work on behalf of LGBTQ equality. We have the power and the spiritual grounding to do more than offer a respite for those who have been bruised or dejected, or are simply distrustful of other faiths. Like Dr. King, we can find the transforming power of our own faith through encounters with the other. We do not need to assert ourselves as the only path to the Divine in the world. But we will find our way as a source of light for others only if we stay committed to our own spiritual deepening. When we take this journey, we will find our place as part of a transformative spirit creating a religiously deep *and* diverse justice-loving world.

—◦—

SHARON GROVES *joined the Religion and Faith staff of the Human Rights Campaign (HRC) in September 2005. She has overseen the creation of numerous new resources, including a weekly preaching resource, a guide to living openly in your place of worship, a curriculum that follows the movie* For the Bible Tells Me So, *and another that helps congregations wrestle with issues of gender identity within their faith communities. She has published a number of articles on such topics as religion and marriage equality, the importance of religious advocacy within the LGBTQ community, and the struggle for equality within world religions. She previously served as managing editor for* Feminist Studies, *an interdisciplinary scholarly journal housed at the University of Maryland, where she also taught courses in English literature, literature and social change, and women's studies. She is a lay leader at All Souls Church, Unitarian, in Washington, D.C., where she has chaired the Committee on Ministry and worked extensively on issues of racial justice, community voting rights, and neighborhood outreach. She has engaged in extensive course work in theology and sexuality from Wesley Theological Seminary* *and the Chicago Theological Seminary. In 2011, Sharon was named director of the HRC Office of Religion and Faith.*

BEYOND EITHER/OR

AMY ZUCKER MORGENSTERN

A woman I once met, when asked when she first knew she was a lesbian, answered unhesitatingly, "age two." I'm not one of those people who have known their sexual orientation all their lives. I didn't get the first glimmer of the idea that I might be bisexual until I was about eighteen, and I didn't strongly identify this way until several years later. There were revelatory moments, such as the one that came when I was watching the opening scene of *Rear Window*. Seeing Grace Kelly's luminous face loom into close-up as she leans in to kiss James Stewart, I was surprised by my emphatic wish, "Kiss me! Kiss me!" On the whole, my realization that I was bi arrived in degrees, a gradual perceptual shift.

What I have known for as long as memory stretches back is that either-or choices make me suspicious. When presented with a confident statement that two things stand on the opposite sides of an unbridgeable divide—material and spiritual, traditional and modern, Israel and Palestine, male and female—I now, by long practice, reflexively ask whether they are really mutually exclusive. What category might encompass them both, synthesize them into a whole? Is there a both/and somewhere? Reading Buddhist philosophy gave a scholarly backing to this ornery tendency, but even before discovering writers who revel in paradox, I always leaned this way; in fact, it's undoubtedly why I took to Zen the moment I encountered its gleeful attitude toward apparent contradictions.

Being a both/and thinker serves me well as a minister, particularly in the role of community builder. Part of my job is finding a way for opposites to dwell together in peace. Theologically, I am committed to moving beyond the choices that are often presented to us as either/or, and

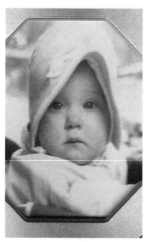

to leading others past those unreal boundaries. I once gave a sermon called "Confessions of a Theist Humanist."

The desire to go beyond either/or also brought me to Unitarian Universalism and has kept me here. Here was a place where I could be Jewish (the religion of my upbringing) *and* Buddhist *and* this great new thing called Unitarian Universalist too—a place where no one would say, "You have to choose one or another." It is a religion that allows room for each of us to fold new ideas into our current theology, practices, and ethical perspective, a religion where the assumption that meets such changes is not "You can't do that" but "Let's see how that fits in!" Unitarian Universalism is the both/and religion, the one that had successfully challenged so many rules of society and theology and shown them to be illusion. Religion will crumble if it admits of skepticism? On the contrary, it will be strengthened, wrote Unitarian Universalist forebears William Ellery Channing, Theodore Parker, and Hosea Ballou. Women can't be leaders, nor even voters, without losing their femininity? Of course they can, said our Unitarian and Universalist suffragists. Atheism undermines morality? Impossible—the well-being of humanity is our core religious concern, said the Unitarian and Universalist signers of the Humanist Manifestos.

Although I hadn't yet discovered Unitarian Universalism, by the end of high school I was well-trained in the habit of taking either/or questions and seeking both/and answers. So when I discovered that the world was not divided into heterosexual and homosexual but included many people who were romantically drawn to both another sex and their own, I already stood on a foundation that made that fact unsurprising, easy to accept, and, ultimately, attractive to apply to myself.

Not that I'm both/and about everything. I believe there are ideas that are mutually exclusive and actions that are incompatible with certain desired outcomes. Much of my ethical base is about delineating, "If you choose A, then B will be necessarily excluded, and C will necessarily follow." I am monogamous not because I'm opposed to polyamory in principle—if people can make it work, all power to them—but because what my wife and I know about ourselves tells us that we are most likely to find what we seek within a single relationship. My Unitarian Universalism encompasses aspects of theism and humanism, and allows me to be both Buddhist/Taoist and Jewish, but it isn't all-inclusive. As much as I admire Christianity and Islam and learn from them, I don't claim them as my own. There are limits to both/and-ness, yet it is one of the gifts we Unitarian Universalists have to offer the world. One of the gifts bisexual people can offer Unitarian Universalism is to help our movement further develop both/and thinking.

When Judaism and I began to part ways and I was seeking a new religious path, one that I never considered was Unitarian Universalism. The reason was simple: Despite growing up in a town with a well-established congregation and passing another on a daily basis, I didn't know such a religion existed. I only knew its name, and I thought it was a Protestant denomination similar to the Presbyterian, Congregational, and Lutheran churches nearby. Nothing I read in the paper or heard about it suggested it might be something quite different. I had been vaguely aware at some point during high school that some friends and schoolmates went to a youth group at the "Unitarian Church"; my reaction was that it must be better than my stereotype of church youth groups, because they were all nice and not fanatical, but it didn't occur to me to go along. The answers I was seeking weren't in Christian churches.

So while I knew the word *Unitarian*, I didn't realize it included anything that I would want to be part of. We were kept apart by a simple misunderstanding.

When I did finally learn enough about Unitarian Universalism to realize that it might be right for me, I had to try it out before I could know for certain. Once I had read a couple of books and went to a couple of services, there was no doubt, and no going back. As so many others have said, I'd been a Unitarian Universalist for years—I just hadn't known it. Now I could live it.

When I joined my first Unitarian Universalist congregation, the Unitarian Universalist Church of Auburn, New York, I inadvertently hurt my mom's feelings by not telling her beforehand about the ceremony, which involved my signing the membership book and receiving a gift. She thought of it as something momentous, a conversion, but I didn't think of it that way. In its way, it was momentous, but it was also just a small, natural step from where I already was. I had realized that what I already was had a name attached to it, and a community, a history, a heritage. It changed everything and nothing.

In the same way, by the time I realized I was that thing called bisexual, the realization no longer carried the drama of revelation. As with Unitarian Universalism, I hadn't really known it existed. I knew some girls who were lesbians, and I thought, "Well, that's not me. I like boys." The both/ and possibility occurred to me only gradually, thanks to the college newsletter's twice-weekly invitation to the LBQ Women group, a few people who identified as bi, and Grace Kelly. If bisexuality had been advertised as badly as Unitarian Universalism, I might have taken even longer to put it all together. But by the time I knew I was attracted to women, I had also, mercifully, learned that others had attractions to both men and women, and that that was called bisexuality.

I couldn't be completely certain that bisexuality and I were a match until I fell in love with a woman for the first time. From that point, it was the most obvious and natural thing in the world. I'd been bi for years—I just hadn't known it.

Unitarian Universalism and bisexuality share the quality of invisibility. It isn't beneficial to either, and perhaps Unitarian Universalists can learn something from bisexuals' dogged insistence on acknowledgment. In the case of bisexuality, invisibility arises from the peculiar rules a please-check-one-and-only-one-box society imposes. It's one half of the double bind that holds us: If we are openly involved with one person, then we are implicitly identifying as either hetero or gay. If, on the other hand, we speak openly about involvements with both men and women, we confirm the stereotype that bisexuals just can't make up their minds, can't be faithful, or are all polyamorous.

Of course, as with so many double binds, the dilemma is caused not by the nature of bisexuality but by the rigidity of social expectations. When we dismiss those rules, the problem dissolves. Just as people in our congregations are learning not to assume that a man who speaks of his partner is referring to a woman, we can learn not to assume that a different-sex relationship means the people involved are hetero, or that a same-sex relationship means the people involved are gay. Bisexuality is always a possibility and, studies suggest, will be increasingly so as we free people to be more candid about their true orientation. We can do that through activism—by removing the real, legal penalties for being openly bi—and through being supportive in our personal relationships with the bi folks who visit, join, and lead our congregations and organizations.

Many bisexual people stay closeted out of fear. Why do Unitarian Universalists? I think it is often for the same reason. We accept the assumptions of the wider society; we define ourselves by its categories, which have no place for the likes of us; and so we become reticent to say, "Actually, there is another option." We closet ourselves. The implications of saying of our religious home, "We are a both/and place" may be scary. For many, such a statement carries pejorative connotations, just as bisexuality does. According to some members of other, more creedal faiths, we Unitarian Universalists are simply unable, or unwilling, to make a commitment. Our diverse approach to spiritual sources, which is one of our great strengths, they interpret as wishy-washiness; we don't stand for anything. We can't commit to one path. And although they are sometimes true, these assumptions miss the larger truth that Unitarian Universalism *is* a path.

To affirm the possibility of both/and is to blaze a new trail, or rather, to clear a trail that many have walked before but that continually becomes overgrown. It can be hard going. Even within Unitarian Universalism, we've internalized many of the either/or messages from other faiths. For many of us, these are the very messages that sent us here to find an alternative in the first place. We question whether our religion is useful to people in poverty, or without advanced formal education, accepting too readily the either/or that says one is either multidegreed or uninterested in subtle ideas. We repeat the old drama of spirituality versus social justice, as if we must be either an activist church or concerned with tending our spirits.

As Unitarian Universalists, we inherit a great legacy from generations of people who heard all the negatives of either/or thinking. To needless prohibitions, they responded, "Why not?" Openly bi people among us can be spiritual leaders in helping us to make the most of that legacy. A heterosexual friend of mine once said, in all seriousness, that he admired those of us who could be attracted to more than one sex—as if we demonstrated a higher spirituality, a kind of open-mindedness that "hopelessly heterosexual" people such as he had not attained. I laughed but strongly disagreed. Bisexuality is not inherently better; for mysterious reasons, human beings have a range of orientations and none is better than the others. We bi folks are just being ourselves. But when the wider society denies that one's self is a true and possible thing, then being one's self is itself an act of courage and spiritual leadership. All openly LGBTQ people among us have led their Unitarian Universalist kin in practicing integrity and wholeness, and we can continue to do so, if others will follow.

Many challenges of either/or thinking still confront Unitarian Universalism. We struggle, still, to say "why not?" to theological diversity, political diversity, class diversity, and racial and ethnic diversity. We struggle even to be open to both children and adults, to both young adults and elders, to both cradle Unitarian Universalists and converts. Bisexuals know just how hard it is to say both/and where others have said either/or. It puts you betwixt and between. Feeling as if you don't belong anywhere isn't easy. People are comfortable with categories and challenged, even frightened, by evidence that the walls separating one category from another are permeable.

But bisexuals have also learned that the problem is not in ourselves but in the categories, which are figments of the mind. Coming out is a proclamation of faith in reality over the divisions that falsely claim authority. Likewise, Unitarian Universalism does best when it comes out and claims its power as a both/and faith.

Several years after coming out to my congregation as bi, I co-authored an adult religious education curriculum on bisexuality. In it, I suggested exercises that would help people move beyond either/or thinking. One of the exercises asks people to go to one side of the room or the other, depending on whether they like vanilla or chocolate, walking alone in nature or being with friends, reading books or listening to music. Being Unitarian Universalists, participants often resist the binary options. Even though the facilitators firmly instruct them to choose one side or the other, almost all gripe about this arbitrary division. Some disregard the rules, invent a continuum, and put themselves somewhere in between.

In other words, Unitarian Universalists are ripe for understanding bisexuality. When they don't get it—and I've encountered some who don't—it's usually because they haven't expanded their capacity for both/and thinking to encompass sexual orientation. I take hope from the fact that most Unitarian Universalists embrace both/and thinking in other areas of their lives.

In general, I've found the people in my congregation accepting of my orientation, blessedly regarding it as a nonissue. The problematic responses, however, have taken three forms: bewilderment, judgment and avoidance, and a flat refusal to acknowledge the reality of bisexuality.

The bewildered response is something like this: "Well, I just don't know about these things," with an implication that they'd rather not. In the old days, everyone was heterosexual, or we thought they were; then we learned that some people were gay, and we're okay with that. But now we have all these other things. Bisexuality, like transgender identity, complicates things. It takes a binary that seemed perfectly clear, black and white, and introduces shades of gray. For some people, gray is confusing.

Judgment and avoidance are closely linked; those few people who have openly articulated harsh judgments of bi—and other queer and genderqueer—members of our congregation have couched their disapproval in questions like "Why do we have to talk about . . . ?" The bugaboo I'd most like to see disappear is the myth that talking about LGBTQ issues equals talking about sex. When someone complains, "Why do we have to talk about sex all the time?," the example often given is someone publicly reminding people that he has a male partner. The issue seems to be generational, a discomfort felt mostly by people of a generation that has been taught not to talk about sex openly. Just the same, there's a double standard. When a hetero couple stands up with shining faces at Caring and Sharing to tell the congregation that they're expecting a baby, we don't complain that they are inappropriately alluding to their sexuality; we congratulate them warmly. We all understand that they weren't leering, "Guess what we did a few months back?" One of the privileges of heterosexuality is the permission to talk about

admittedly sexual relationships without anyone construing such talk as embarrassingly private.

I want to claim for myself and other LGBTQ people—within our congregations and everywhere—the same both/and that most heterosexuals take for granted: that of being sexual and having a life that goes far beyond physical sex. Although our sexuality defines part of who we are, that doesn't mean that at any given moment we are doing, or even thinking about, anything sexual. (I'm the parent of a young child. When I get into bed, what I'm hankering after is sleep.) As with most people of whatever sexuality who are not currently in the hormonal storms of adolescence or newly in love, my identity is less about what I do than who and what I am. I'm a human, a woman, a person of European heritage, a U.S. citizen, a Unitarian Universalist, a bisexual. I will still be bi even if I remain in the same relationship for the rest of my life, as I ardently hope I will. I would have been bi even if I had had relationships only with men or only with women.

The "bisexuality doesn't exist" response takes a subtle form: the assumption that self-declared bisexuals are really something else. I was asked by one woman, sympathetically but exasperatingly, whether I was "in transition." I so misunderstood the lingo that it took me a week to realize she was asking whether I was just taking a step on the way to admitting I was a lesbian. I don't generally mind being taken for a lesbian—it's an honorable title—but I do mind the corollaries: first, that I'm lying when I describe myself as bi, and second, that my first marriage, which was to a man, broke up because our orientations were incompatible. In fact, my former husband knew I was bi and couldn't have cared less. The assumption that a woman attracted to women felt bound to leave a heterosexual marriage makes sense if you ignore bisexuality and insist that the only options are "exclusively heterosexual" and "exclusively homosexual."

In a similar vein, I've had someone in the church's LGBTQ community suggest that another bi person—in fact, our other minister—was not a true member of that community because she was married to a man. In other words, I got a pass because I had a girlfriend (now my wife) and therefore resembled a lesbian. Likewise, many hetero people in the congregation simply didn't register that their other minister, who had spoken clearly of her bisexuality from the pulpit, was bi. It was easy for them to disregard her membership among the LGBTQ community even when she proclaimed it, because she was married to a man. In each case, people struggled to acknowledge the both/and before their eyes: that we bisexuals fit into neither category, gay/lesbian nor hetero, but are something outside that either/or.

—◦—

AMY ZUCKER MORGENSTERN *has been parish minister of the Unitarian Universalist Church of Palo Alto, California, since 2003, having previously served the congregations in Rutland*

and Middlebury, Vermont. Her vision of Unitarian Universalism is expressed in the mission of her congregation: "Transforming ourselves, each other, and the world." Always an activist, she was propelled into action for LGBTQ rights by the Vermont debate that resulted in the nation's first civil unions law. She has a passion for adult religious education, has taught the subject at the Starr King School for the Ministry, and in 2007 coauthored Interweave Continental's bisexuality curriculum. An artist, Amy posts her works-in-progress and writes about religion, politics, and culture at her blog, Sermons in Stones. She lives in San Francisco with her wife, Joy, and their four-year-old daughter.

SAVED BY LOVE

MICHAEL TINO

The first time I attended a Unitarian Universalist church for worship, I was greeted by an incredible sight: 75 percent of the congregation were wearing pink triangles on their name tags. I didn't know what to make of it. I thought I'd died and gone to some sort of queer heaven.

I remember vividly looking around me and seeing all of the triangles. I wouldn't have guessed he was "family," I thought to myself, or her. That man and woman sitting together holding hands—I guess they could be bisexual. And that older couple with the same last name—maybe they came out to each other later in life and stayed married for reasons beyond sexual attraction. Good for them. Good for all of them.

I didn't want to assume that people were straight. After all, they had their pink triangles on, proudly proclaiming their queer identity. And who was I to argue with people's self-identification? So I made myself right at home amidst the pink triangle–bedecked crowd.

I sat there in wonder through the service as the female minister—also wearing a pink triangle—preached about the feminine face of the Divine. At the time, I was a twenty-one-year-old gay New Yorker new to the South (albeit the citified, yuppified, Yankeefied South of Durham, North Carolina). Moreover, I was a third-generation lapsed Catholic who had long ago given up the notion that there would ever be a religious community that accepted my distinctly unorthodox theology, much less my sexuality.

During coffee hour, someone finally explained to me that, in a worship several months before, the congregation had been challenged to wear a pink triangle whatever their sexual orientation. They were informed about the origin of the pink triangle to mark gay men in Nazi Germany, and told the story of the King of Denmark, who, in that era, wore a yellow Star of David even though he wasn't Jewish.

At first, I was disappointed. After all, I'd thought I had landed in a queer parallel universe. But the more I thought about it, the more I was amazed by this group of people who were willing to be perceived as gay, lesbian, or bisexual to send a welcoming message to those of us who actually were queer. The more I thought about it, the more I realized that I had experienced radical hospitality at its finest, and that was something even more awesome than a church full of queer folks.

Although I had many amazing heterosexual friends who step up as allies to LGBT folks again and again, I had never before encountered an institution that made such a statement. I had not encountered many straight people who were willing to wear a pink triangle without a disclaimer, such as "straight but not narrow." Yet there I was, faced with an entire congregation of people whose simple act of affixing a pink triangle sticker to their name tags changed the course of my life. This wasn't the first time Unitarian Universalists had changed my life—but it was the first time I knew it.

I grew up in a warm, loving Italian-American family in the New York City of the seventies and eighties. Think of the movie *Moonstruck*, but in a less fancy section of Brooklyn, and you're pretty much there. My family expressed love easily and often. I was never given cause to doubt the breadth or depth of my parents' love. Although life in the Tino household certainly had its ups and downs over the years, on the balance there were a whole lot more ups.

In my family, it has always been possible to talk about almost anything. We debate and argue regularly. To this day, it is not unusual to hear talk about sex at the dinner table with my family of origin. We still vividly recall the day my grandmother (the most traditional Italian Catholic in the family), then in her eighties, proclaimed

that sex with my grandfather wasn't much good once he hit ninety. I am profoundly grateful for my family.

Part of growing up in New York City is being exposed to an amazing variety of people. Every shade of the human rainbow is present on a typical subway ride, as is every language spoken by the human tongue or hands. Within such diversity, it is pretty much impossible not to learn something of gay, lesbian, bisexual, and transgender people. Although consciousness of sexual orientation was slowly growing elsewhere in America through the seventies and eighties, it was pretty much in full bloom in New York. A simple nighttime ride up Manhattan's West Side Highway took one past leather bars and transvestite prostitutes. My family took this route on the average Friday night, on the way to the Catskills after picking my dad up from his office in the Woolworth Building. Although most people would have sped by the Ramrod without a comment, my parents never pretended that the people we saw outside our car did not exist. However, I was smart enough to know that, despite the giggles over the name of that bar, its patrons were not acceptable. My parents, who were clearly more liberal-minded than most people I knew, were clearly not in favor of queer folks being public about who they were. The rest of society was even worse, of course. I knew about homophobia by the time I was twelve; I had been paying attention all along to how others reacted to people like me. I heard too many comments to count about "fags" and "dykes." I vividly recall the revulsion many people expressed when Billie Jean King publicly came out in the early eighties. I remember friends wondering aloud about gay male sex: "If two men are in a relationship with each other, which one is 'the woman' when they do it?" I sat silently and wide-eyed through seventh-grade health class when the class reacted (loudly, badly, hideously) to our teacher's assertion that two men or two women having sexual intercourse with each other was perfectly normal. In the midst of figuring out what all of these messages had to do with me, I was scared out of my mind, like so many, by the news that gay men were dying of a strange new disease called AIDS.

Faced with these messages from everyone around me, I decided that I had no choice but to hide who I was. I was not willing to risk being rejected by my family. I was not willing to risk losing my friends. I was not willing to risk being forced into the margins of society. I was not willing to risk being trapped in an identity that was dangerous, despised, and abnormal (no matter what Mrs. Levinson had to say in health class). I was not willing to abandon the dreams a young person has of having a career, a family, and a stable home.

Most of all, I saw clearly that nobody who was open about their queer sexuality was happy. Billie Jean King lost all of her endorsements and got sued by an ex- when she came out in 1981. Gay men apparently faced a death sentence just for having sex. There were no role models, no icons, no real people I could point to who were successful, healthy, happy, "normal," and gay.

In retrospect, I am thankful that I never got the message that I should fear hell, on top of rejection by my family and society in general. Damnation was not on the Tino family radar, although spirituality of different sorts was. I understood why my parents, and most of my grandparents, had rejected Catholicism. I saw my mother's struggles with hypocrisy in her brief time as a Jehovah's Witness. I understood that I had to carve out my own spiritual niche in the world, and it would not be long before I had developed my own version of universalist theology. I could not believe in a God whose capacity for love and forgiveness was as small as most of Christianity made it out to be. It took years, however, to realize that I wasn't the only one.

As a teenager, I found it quite easy to hide my identity at first by ignoring it altogether. I poured myself into justice and service work in high school, working tirelessly to feed the homeless and raise funds for famine relief in Africa. I organized educational events and lots of fundraisers ending in "-a-thon." I organized efforts to lobby local congresspeople on issues such as foreign aid, global disease prevention, and domestic poverty relief. I spent weekends sleeping on the floor of a Friends meetinghouse in Manhattan and working in food pantries, homeless shelters, and "welfare hotels." For a long while, I could easily pretend that nothing having to do with sex or sexuality had anything to do with me. I had so many friends that not having a girlfriend wasn't especially odd. I was busy enough saving the world that no one cared that I never dated. I studied hard and got good grades. Yet ignoring my feelings got harder and harder. I was, after all, a teenager, and my body and mind were conspiring to make me keenly aware of my desires.

Faced with both the inability to act on those desires and the overwhelming sense that something was very wrong with me, I became depressed—at times suicidal. I was lonely, despite my many close friends, my robust family, and my service work. It's hard to think about that time without tearing up at the thought of being a sixteen-year-old on a subway platform, staring into the darkness and seeing no hope, no light, and no future.

It was during my service weekends at the Friends meetinghouse that I met Alice, who was then a first-year college student and a Quaker. Alice and I shared an oddball sense of humor, a fondness for writing letters, and a strange fascination with the mashed potatoes at the diner around the block from the meetinghouse. We both spent weekend after weekend serving others, and we became fast friends. One bright, sunny Saturday afternoon, Alice and I were charged with taking the children from a "welfare hotel" in Midtown Manhattan to the North Bronx, so they could play in Van Cortlandt Park. That day, I was forced to rethink everything I thought I knew about sexuality and identity, everything I had concluded about my future.

It was a long ride from Manhattan to the Bronx on the number 1 train. We had plenty of help making sure the kids behaved on the subway ride, so Alice and I started to talk. Just about when the train emerged from underground,

Alice told me about someone she knew who had come out as a lesbian. I was shocked. As the subway car emerged into the brilliant sunlight, though, I learned the part of the story that would change my life: This person was happy. Happier than she had ever been in her life. Happy that she could date whom she wanted, happy that she was no longer living a lie, happy that she could be herself.

I was amazed. I'd never heard of such a thing. Imagine— a happy lesbian! I'm sure I expressed my shock to Alice, because she explained to me that all of the people she knew who were lesbian, gay, or bisexual were much happier after coming out. All of them? More than one? Some were men? As the train lurched northward carrying our precious cargo of homeless children, I knew my life had been changed.

Although Alice and I remained pen pals through college, our letters tapered off when I hit graduate school, and we lost touch for almost a decade. We reconnected when we bumped into each other at a Unitarian Universalist Association (UUA) General Assembly, an annual meeting of our congregations attended by several thousand people. We were both, as it turned out, in seminary. Although neither of us was a Unitarian Universalist in the late eighties, by the early years of the twenty-first century, we had not only found the same religion but had also heard and accepted its call to ministry. Alice, now Rev. Alice Anacheka-Nasemann, is today a colleague in the Unitarian Universalist ministry.

I told Alice the subway story recently, and she was amazed at the effect her simple words had had on me. She knew—and was happy—that I had come out since high school and that my life was good and full, but she had no idea of the profound role she had played in showing me that happiness was a possibility for me.

As I headed off to college, I was no longer hopeless and depressed; I was merely confused. Alice's story had saved my life—I shudder to think how literally. I finally had heard of others who had embraced their sexuality and emerged happier and stronger people. I was still not sure if I could join them, though, because I could not reconcile these stories with my carefully crafted fantasy future of career and family. Although the first cracks had appeared in my armor of pretend heterosexuality, it would take more than a few cracks for me to shed the suit completely.

During my first year in college, controversy erupted in my residence hall when a dance party was advertised with a silhouette of a man and woman dancing. The dorm's staff labeled the posters heterosexist and would not let the dance organizers put them up. Heated arguments ensued, the dance organizers not understanding what they could possibly have done wrong. It was a couple dancing, and no offense was intended. And what was this "heterosexism" thing, anyway? None of us had ever heard that term before.

As a first-year student on the program council, I had no idea what to make of the uproar. I simply could not believe that anyone would be open enough about their sexuality to bring a same-sex date to a dorm-wide dance. Did men really dance with other men? Women with other women? Further, the fact that the staff thought this issue was important enough to protest was a revelation—people I respected and admired insisted that we had to take gay, lesbian, and bisexual people into account. *Crack.*

Not long after that, a close friend came out to me. Ian's response to the ugly arguments over the dance posters was to come to terms with his own sexual orientation, and that meant telling his friends. I remember vividly—we sat in my dorm room talking, and I stared at Ian in disbelief. I remember thinking, "I can't believe I'm a close enough friend to tell this to," and, more important, "I can't imagine what it would take for me to tell someone else that I'm gay too." *Crack.*

Little by little, I knew I was approaching the time when I would confront my sexuality. By sophomore year, I knew I could not last much longer in the closet. I was terrified, to say the least. Would I still have friends when it was over? What would my parents and family say? And what would become of my carefully planned future? I froze in panic, unable to contemplate the answers to these questions.

What finally got the armor to come off for good was a song—a song, as it turns out, by a Unitarian Universalist, although I didn't know it at the time. Sometime during my sophomore year in college, a friend gave me a cassette tape of Fred Small's album *No Limit.* Halfway through the album is the now-iconic song "Everything Possible," which I had never heard before. By the end of the song, I was in tears.

It seems kind of corny to me twenty years later, but this simple song of love and hope opened my eyes and my heart in a way that nothing else had. That Fred sang of same-sex love among the things possible in life meant that I heard myself, for the first time ever, included in a song. I was included. No longer cast off to the margins. No longer forgotten, ignored, or rejected. No longer the freak on the corner or the teenager staring into the darkness. Everything was possible *for me*.

Although my coming-out process had its fits and starts, that song set me on the path to where I am today. Over time, I told my friends, who remained loving and supportive and close. In time, I told my family, who, after many tears and much work, came to love that part of me I had kept hidden for so long. I've seen my share of discrimination and heard my share of homophobic insults, but coming out ushered integrity and authenticity into my life, and helped me become whole.

Fred is now a fellow Unitarian Universalist minister. The world, as it turns out, is a very small place, and our faith and its saving message of love found me again and again in my hours of need, well before I came to know myself as a Unitarian Universalist. I've had the chance to thank

Fred in person for his song, after he sang it at another UUA General Assembly. We cried together that night—tears of joy and gratitude. I'm sure I'm not the only one whose life was changed because he made them feel normal for the first time.

As I sat in the sanctuary at the Eno River Unitarian Universalist Fellowship in early 1994, Unitarian Universalism saved me again. There, amidst all of the pink triangles, I realized that the possibilities for my life included being a religious person. Since my childhood, I had had room for spirituality in my life, but I had long since given up hope that my spirituality could be expressed in religious community. Being invited to a Unitarian Universalist congregation changed that. Finding one in which the members went out of their way to make sure I knew I was welcome was the first step.

The pink triangles helped me decide that I had found a spiritual home, but there was more. At Eno River, I found a place where I was not merely tolerated or accepted for who I was but appreciated for it. Where every part of me—my sexual orientation no less than my theology, my scientific background, and my experience working with children and youth—was valued and celebrated.

The weekend after signing the membership book, I found myself at a teacher training for the *About Your Sexuality* curriculum, a comprehensive sexuality curriculum taught in Unitarian Universalist congregations from 1969 to 1999, when it was replaced by *Our Whole Lives*. I had been a member for five days, and already I was being asked to help create a safe, positive environment for seventh and eighth graders to learn about sexuality in a healthy way. After receiving so many gifts from Unitarian Universalists and Unitarian Universalism, I was being asked to be the role model for youth and help them to know that their own sexuality was valued and appreciated. My ministry had begun.

Over the next five years, I would realize my own calling to the Unitarian Universalist ministry. It happened while I was working with teenagers at the Southeast Unitarian Universalist Summer Institute, a week-long intergenerational camp held on a college campus in western Virginia. I was part of a staff of adults whose job it was to create a safe space in which over a hundred teens could be themselves and be loved just the way they were. For one week a year, these young people knew there was nothing wrong with them. For some, it was the only week they had ever experienced such radical acceptance.

I got to witness and facilitate transformations that I imagine were not too different from mine, if sometimes less painful. I watched as the walls fell away from the hearts of teens used to keeping up strong defenses. I saw them open up when they were shown (and not just told) that they were beautiful, whole, good, and loved. I realized that ministers had the awesome task of creating a space where people of all ages felt that way not just one week a year but all the time. That was when I first considered professional leadership in this religion that had saved my life again and again, this faith that had made it possible for me to be whole, love myself, and be loved.

In the call to help create communities of radical hospitality, inclusion, wholeness, and healing, I heard my call to the ministry. In following that call, I pledged to work for the salvation of our world, a salvation that is possible only when all of us know the depth and breadth of love that is available to us without condition.

⊸◦⊶

MICHAEL TINO *is the minister of the Unitarian Universalist Fellowship of Northern Westchester in Mount Kisco, New York. Born and raised in New York City, Michael lived in Durham, North Carolina, for fifteen years before returning to the New York metro area. He now lives in Peekskill, New York, with his partner of eleven years, Eric. Michael is the proud uncle of three amazing young people he hopes will grow up knowing that they are just right the way they are. Michael holds a BS from Cornell University, a PhD in cell biology from Duke University, and an MDiv from Meadville/Lombard Theological School. He currently serves as president of the Unitarian Universalist Allies for Racial Equity and is deeply involved in anti-racism, anti-oppression, and justice-making work throughout the movement. He was ordained to the ministry in 2007.*

Everything Broken and Whole

Sunshine Jeremiah Wolfe

You cannot have wholeness without brokenness. To be at peace with the universe, or what some call G-d, is to encompass all—the broken and the whole. In Unitarian Universalism, I found a whole that could welcome all of me despite the brokenness within Unitarian Universalism, or perhaps even because of it. I am genderqueer. To even be able to say that or describe what that means for me, I had to become a Unitarian Universalist and, through this powerful religion, discover that as broken and afraid as I was, there are places where all of my being is welcome. Unitarian Universalism helped me trust my mind and open my heart.

Unitarian Universalism has given me language and resolve. I have spoken at dozens of colleges, medical facilities, churches, and community events on being genderqueer and what it's like to be a LGBTQQIA (lesbian, gay, bisexual, transgender, queer, questioning, intersex, and ally) person. In these settings, being able to talk about love as a radical ethical value and sharing the importance of respect for differing ideas has helped significantly. I knew these things before joining a church, but when I speak to total strangers, some of whom judge me based on their religious values, I know that I have a community of ancestors and people standing with me as I speak. It makes a world of difference to know that our values can bring a little grace into the world.

It wasn't a worship service, small group ministry, or pastoral visit that brought me to Unitarian Universalism, although I have certainly found healing in all of those places. The greatest healing came from the Unitarian Universalist Association's comprehensive *Our Whole Lives* sexuality class for adults. The sexologist leading our class said, "I want each of you to decide if you are male, female, or gender neutral. We will go around the circle and share our answers." I remember tears forming in my eyes and the sounds of the world seemed muffled. I thought, "Gender neutral? I can choose gender neutral?" I felt myself trembling and knew with every ounce of my being that this language described who I was. Not only did I get to proclaim in this class that I was gender neutral, but I also discovered that another person in the room identified this way. I wasn't alone! Thus began a road to healing and wholeness that has been a wild ride. Piecing together the broken pieces that make up my gender wholeness took six years, and some gaps may never be filled. That's okay though. Love fills those holes and sustains the spirit of my life.

I grew up in rural Indiana, where gender deviation was not accepted. I had strong female role models, including my grandmother and mother. It was perfectly acceptable in my family for women to have more "masculine" traits. I was able to pass as a strong girl and not worry too much about who I was. I played with trains, Barbie dolls, toy tools, blocks, Strawberry Shortcake, and Hot Wheels cars. I learned that I could play with and be whoever I wanted in my parents' home. Although my parents did not enforce stereotypical gender rules, I learned what I was supposed to be from other family members, school, media, and society.

The only example of a genderqueer/transgender person I knew was a woman with a beard who lived on my street. Kids threw rocks and eggs at her house and yelled obscenities at her. In high school, people made fun of me for being the only girl in the small engine repair class. One teacher told me that I would never get into college preparatory programs if I took technology classes. Television accounts of violence toward those who were "different" told me that troubling the gender waters was not only bad but dangerous.

In college, I came out as bisexual and fell in love with a woman for the first time. This relationship terrified me. Only after years of therapy, self-reflection, and study did I begin to realize that something was different about me—something nameless and well beyond my understanding. I knew only that, if I kept on this path, I would lose my family. I did not want that, so I buried myself in drugs and alcohol for a couple of years. When I sobered up, I substituted another addiction, working constantly. At the heart of this pain was fear that my family would never accept me and that I did not fit into the middle-class world I was supposed to move into. Where would I find home? Who would accept me?

I knew my mother would support me no matter what. Her family is big, and I know all of my great aunts and uncles, first cousins, second cousins, and third cousins. Mom taught me that family was crucial in finding employment, housing, money when you are desperate, support in the bad times, and joy in the good times. My family was and is everything to me.

So I decided to just not deal with whatever was going on within me. For many years, I dated only men and avoided the constant dissonance that played itself out when gender expectations were thrown in my face. A man would take a heavy box from me, and I would get mad. I would insist on paying my own way on a date. More than once, I was told that someone was not comfortable dating me because he didn't feel I was feminine enough. "You should wear dresses more," men told me, or "You should wear makeup."

I would insist that I wanted children but never to give birth. Frequently, my questioning of cultural gender expectations was chalked up to my age, even well into my thirties. "Oh, you will grow out of it." In the United States, we are clearly expected, as we get older, to fit into one of two categories, and always the one associated with our genitals.

Many women are berated for not wearing makeup, showing no interest in bearing children, and struggling with outdated social norms. But as a genderqueer person, I never considered these criticisms an affront to me as a woman. I never felt comfortable calling myself a feminist because feminism and the increasing freedom for women did not answer questions about *my* body and *my* experience. Feminism gave me freedom to defend myself as someone perceived as a woman, but when I did so, I felt like I was being dishonest.

Many of my friends and family assumed that my failure to conform meant that I was a lesbian. I have never identified as a lesbian. I have always found people of all genders and sexual orientations attractive. Bisexual and pansexual people often run into this form of discrimination, and for years, I felt frustrated that others' assumptions about my sexual orientation had to do with their ignorance about bisexual and pansexual people.

I could find no solid images, words, or examples of what I was, and therefore, I was lost. My heart was filled with pain and confusion. Nothing in my education talked about genderqueer people. My friends who were bisexual, gay, lesbian, and transgender did not talk about genderqueer identity. Nothing in the media portrayed anything remotely related to my experiences as genderqueer. I didn't know what I was, so I ignored my body.

In Unitarian Universalism, I faced some of my most painful experiences—and ultimately found my spiritual home.

I was raised in a mixed-religion family. My father is an atheist, my mother lives in the Tsa-La-Gi and Dakota ways, and my grandparents took me to their Catholic church. In addition, my mother ensured that I had exposure to many religious traditions, including Taoism, Sufism, paganism, and Protestant Christianity. I often joke that I was raised a Unitarian Universalist without the church.

I joined my first Unitarian Universalist church after college in March 2000. My love for Unitarian Universalism was instant. In particular, the Principles and Purposes really spoke to me. At its best, Unitarian Universalism is a religion of people who covenant to treat one another well, care for the earth, and protect the beautiful tapestry of cultures and communities that make up the people of the world. Love is the core value from which we build. Of course, none of this is easy. We struggle and stumble and fall. As Rev. Dr. Sharon Welch has written, "We are, quite simply, like all the generations before us, and all the generations that will come after, learning to walk."

As a Unitarian Universalist, I believe in heaven here on earth and that each of us has responsibility for caring for each other. My friend Ulysses once told me about a conversation he had with a Christian friend. Our church was at the height of conflict over something, and he was sharing his concerns. His friend asked, "What keeps you in your church?" He said, "We are a religious community that is committed to one another. I have faith that we as people can work it out." "Wow, I couldn't do that," she replied. "I have to have faith in God because I don't have faith that people can work it out." Unitarian Universalists' belief that we must do the work has kept me in this religion when I wanted only to run out the door.

Our Unitarian Universalist communities have growing edges. Among the most difficult interactions for me as a genderqueer person are those with people who think they can intellectually judge me as acceptable or not. Meeting someone whose first response to something they know little or nothing about is humility and open ears is truly a joy.

One time the Young Adult Group at my church had a workshop about what women's bodies tell us about spirituality. Women in the group talked about the power to create, the ebb and flow of the cycles of the moon, and the power of female divine symbols in their lives. I remember thinking that this was interesting, but I could not relate to any of the commentary. Then came my turn. I answered honestly, "I think bodies have a lot to do with spirituality, but there is nothing in particular about my being a woman that informs that." The group leader was not happy with my response. Her deep anger and dismissive attitude in what I had perceived as a safe space really jostled something within me.

I was not quite sure what had happened. I went about my days but kept coming back to this question: What does my body tell me about spirituality? I wasn't sure, but I was sure the answer was important.

The leader of that group discussion had cracked the door open to something I had pushed away for at least twenty years. Feeling confused, I talked to my therapist about my experience and the questions it had raised. He said it was common for women to push away their bodies and gave me exercises that were meant to help me find my power as a woman. The exercises only led to frustration on my part and his. I stopped going to therapy with him. I wish I could say that I turned to my minister or other church friends or leaders for help during this time, but I did not feel safe or wise doing so. Although many in my congregation are welcoming and try to understand, others are uncomfortable and even rude; some just avoid me altogether.

In 2005, I enrolled in Starr King School for the Ministry. Every year, students sing, "Come, Come Whoever You Are" and then cross the threshold into the school. For the first time in my life, I felt safe enough to talk about what it means to be a genderqueer, pansexual, working-class, multiracial, fat, young-adult, temporarily able-bodied person in the United States. I still had moments that were difficult, but overall I felt a liberation within myself and a trust in my colleagues that I had never fully known before. The school has transgender bathroom signs, out genderqueer faculty, and, at least while I was there, transgender students. I was excited and hopeful, even though I still ran into the assumption that I was female.

One particular moment completely changed my view of my gender. I was taking a Unitarian Universalist theology class, and one of the older students made a comment that women tend to do X and men tend to do Y. I said I thought their comment supported stereotypes and ignored genderqueer people like me. Another student told me that I was wrong and to have respect for my elders. I was enraged but kept silent.

Later that day, my therapist role-played the interaction with me and then asked, "Why did this hurt you so much?" I had to stop and think. After a few moments, I finally spoke the words that I had been afraid to say for years: "Because I don't exist. My experience is totally ignored." To finally proclaim that my body, heart, and spirit are not talked about, recognized, or even known to everyday society was liberating. After further discussions with my therapist, I made the decision to officially come out of the closet as pansexual and genderqueer, to change my name, and to ask people to use the gender-neutral pronouns *ghe* and *gher* in reference to me.

One thing I love about ministry and Unitarian Universalism is the value we place on ritual. After deciding to come out, I asked four of my classmates to create a ritual of transition to which I invited my friends, colleagues, and classmates. I felt such a sense of love from them. The affirmation I experienced from that ritual has carried me through when I succumb to loneliness and fear.

I have a lot to fear. Physical safety is always a concern. Not long after my transition ritual, I was stopped by a man in a parking garage. If his son hadn't asked him to stop, I am sure he would have hit me. My doctor freaked out when I told her I was genderqueer transgender and made errors on routine procedures. I have been followed, denied service at restaurants, and had strangers ask, "What are you?" I have friends who have committed suicide because they are genderqueer and/or transgender. I have a friend whose loved one was murdered for being transgender.

Social safety is also a concern. At the time I am writing, employment and housing discrimination is perfectly legal. As a Unitarian Universalist candidate minister, I know that transgender ministers have had difficulty succeeding in our congregations. How will they respond to someone who is genderqueer, pansexual, *and* transgender?

I love ministry. I feel deep connection in preaching, energizing church communities, fostering lay leadership, and walking with church members during major life transitions such as weddings and illness. My call to ministry lies at the heart of my commitment to living. I enjoy serving something larger than myself, and I enjoy fostering community and supporting individual transformation. However, much of my enjoyment can be overshadowed by church members' discomfort with genderqueer and transgender identity. I have had people walk out of worship when I talk about gender-neutral pronouns, because they do not believe that genderqueer people should be ministers. My financial future is far from secure simply because of who I am.

Within Unitarian Universalist churches, transgender and genderqueer people struggle to explain why our concerns may need to be addressed separately from gay and lesbian concerns, and how our concerns are even different. As a result, activism in our communities typically is limited to singular events at the time of crisis rather than an overall commitment to ensuring security and basic human rights.

Currently, I am a candidate for being called by a Unitarian Universalist congregation as their minister. I have visited many churches for interviews. In every church I have visited, I have met someone who is genderqueer and/or transgender. In all but a few, these members are in the closet in their own church communities. They have friends within the church whom they may be out to, but they are not comfortable telling the congregation. They sneak me business cards or e-mail me after church to maintain their safety. Their behavior says a lot about what it means to be genderqueer and/or transgender in Unitarian Universalism.

Since the 1970 General Assembly Resolution to End Discrimination Against Homosexuals and Bisexuals, Unitarian Universalists have done a lot of good healing work in order to welcome gay and lesbian people. However, I believe we have made the mistake of assuming that education about sexuality will lead to awareness and understanding of gender. Often the two intersect, but understanding sexuality does not necessarily lead to understanding gender, particularly in the lives of transgender and genderqueer people.

So, long ago, I asked the question: What does my body tell me about spirituality? I think everyone should ask themselves this question. There are multiple answers. Above the doors at West Shore Unitarian Universalist Church, the sign reads, "One Church, Many Paths." It could just as easily read, "One Community, Many Bodies." These vessels that are our only permanent homes from birth to death tell us a lot about the spirit that lives within us.

What does my body tell me about spirituality? It reminds me that either/or thinking can divide something that is both/and in nature. As Rita Nakashima Brock writes, "Interstitial spaces are real places." My body teaches me that in-between is a sacred place.

Daily, my body reminds me of the preciousness of living. Lack of physical and social safety constantly reminds me of the gratitude I have for a house to live in and for another day on this earth. My body constantly reminds me of the importance of love. Love bonds me to my family even as we struggle with the very different ways we live. Love guides my religious faith into engagement with the social justice issues of our time. Love keeps me coming to the table when it feels like everything has fallen apart.

My genderqueer body reminds me that interstitial space is constantly in motion, in process. The process of my life has taught me that every moment matters. Embracing the times of my brokenness, when I feel like my pain, fear, or loneliness will swallow me, is as important as embracing the times of my fullness, when I know joy, love, and connection. Often, I hold these supposedly opposite experiences at the same time. They are, in reality, moments of spiritual grace.

In holding both my brokenness and fullness, I have found some of the most grounding and whole experiences in my life. Bodies contain so much that can guide and inform us. If we can come from a place of listening and humbleness, we open ourselves to the divinity of all bodies—all people—billions of unique answers to what it means to be alive, holy, broken, and whole.

◄o►

SUNSHINE JEREMIAH WOLFE, *a graduate of Starr King School for the Ministry in Berkeley, California, recently completed an intern and summer ministry at West Shore Unitarian Universalist Church in Rocky River, Ohio. Sunshine is genderqueer and asks that people use the nongender pronouns* ghe *and* gher *in reference to gherself. The "gh" is pronounced like the "g" in* beige. *Ghe discovered the call to ministry while serving the Unitarian Universalist Church of Tucson as their spiritual development director. Sunshine brings to gher ministry a love for community, deep care for those who need pastoral support, and* *a commitment to creating beloved community through healthy communication and resisting oppression. Ghe is originally from Indiana, where ghe learned to love the earth, sing, and treasure family. Sunshine is a member of Diverse and Revolutionary Unitarian Universalist Multicultural Ministries and Transgender Religious Professional Unitarian Universalists Together.*

Love May Not Be Concerned

Rowan McDowell Thompson

In her poem "Love Is Not Concerned," Alice Walker expresses perfectly my relationship to my faith. I hear her say that God will not only love me regardless of who I am but that God will love me *because* of who I am. God is not concerned about my attempts and failures at being perfect but rather that I try to love as I am loved, wholly and deeply. I have not arrived at this conclusion suddenly and it isn't the end of my spiritual quest, like the resolution of an action-filled adventure story. Instead, I am still living the story, sorting through fallacies and wisdom in search of some castaway truth. But my spiritual story did have a beginning; it started long after my first inklings of love.

Like many people, I had my first crush when I was very little. Her name was Grace; that still seems oddly prophetic to me. Then Leo, Jordan, Maddie, Justin, Shayla, Jane, and Alex came and went from my life. It didn't seem at all odd to me that men would love men and women would love women, because many in my family and my close church community were in same-gender relationships. Their love seemed both beautiful and natural, and I never questioned its validity. Girls feeling sexually attracted to girls, however, didn't seem right to me at all as soon as I hit puberty. Because I didn't find the people I loved attractive and didn't feel love for those I was attracted to, love and attraction never seemed entirely related. For a long time, I felt gross and cut off for being sexually interested in women because what I felt didn't seem the same as the love I had accepted as completely healthy my whole life.

Between exposure to queer culture like *Rocky Horror Picture Show* and participating in the middle-school *Our Whole Lives* (OWL) Unitarian Universalist sexuality education program, I realized that sex was part of being gay and immediately did a 180. Suddenly I identified completely with the sexualized image I had of what it meant to be queer. I was gay, and I wanted to kiss girls, and be hot to girls, and I wanted every gay girl to know that's how I felt. Waves of depression rolled in and out as I began to accept myself, not as a lesbian (I never have identified with that word) but as sexually attracted to women. Then I felt isolated by the lack of any girls my age to be interested in; it seemed that everyone was straight or scared.

As I started high school, I was inspired by two openly queer members of the student body council. I had come out as gay to several close friends, my parents and godmother, and a few friends from church, but I wasn't sharing anything about my sexual self with my school. I had an itch to know more people like me my age and finally met a few kids through a group called BGLAD (Bisexual Gay Lesbian Adolescent Drop-in). BGLAD is a therapy group put together for queer teens by a local organization called Youth Eastside Services. But still I ached for romance—who doesn't in high school? I dated a senior who made me feel on edge at all times that she was going to out me to the school. I couldn't talk to my family because they had specifically told me not to date until I was at least fifteen, and I was still fourteen. So I let her push me around, until eventually she told me she was going to come out to her parents and move out. She wanted me to live with her. I told her there was no way I could do that, so she ended our relationship. I felt terrible and melancholy for a week or two, but eventually I realized how out of balance our pseudo-relationship was; it was based on my desperation

for some kind of romantic contact with another queer girl. Like so many things in life, in retrospect it seems idiotic, but at the time I was doing my best.

Fortunately, the summer after ninth grade, an acquaintance from BGLAD invited me to go with hir to a week-long activism camp in Olympia, our state capital. Ze and I stayed in a house with several complete strangers who shared the house communally. These young adults embodied a way of living that I much admired: They were queer and sex-positive, allies to youth, aware of and involved with food ethics, not materialists, and fighting homelessness in their community. They were also movie, book, and music buffs who shared a deep love of visual art. They loved each other even when they didn't like each other. The camp itself, Stonewall Activism Summer School, was created by and for queer young people who are activists. I was introduced to a whole new concept of queer culture and what it means to be a queer person in America. Ze became my best friend and helped me redefine my sexual self. As a genderqueer kid, Ze introduced me to a more fluid way of being and taught me that I don't need to define myself by who I'm attracted to. I can just be attracted to people, and it's only whose business I make it. My friend held me accountable to a standard of love, not image. Love is not concerned with whom I find sexy; love is concerned that I should not beat myself with a word that tears up my soul. Since when can a person be summed up in one word anyway?

So far, choosing to describe myself as queer has only opened doors for me. Nonetheless, I'd use many more words, like quirky, camper, cook, musician, activist, movie-lover, reader, storyteller, lover-of-laughing, peer sex educator, Unitarian Universalist, follower of Jesus, daughter, cousin, and friend. All of these characteristics are core to who I am, but the enabler for everything else has always been that I am a person of faith. Growing up in the Unitarian Universalist tradition has instilled in me deep values that I carry through every aspect of my life. These values can be found in our seven Principles and in our way of creating community. In my experience, though, strong values alone are not sufficient. I have struggled with doubt most of my life, and that feeling of uncertainty has not been what carried me through dark times. When I was in the depths of despair, whether caused by internal chemical imbalance or external emotional imbalance, values weren't good enough. I needed faith. So began my search for a tradition that both reflected my values and expressed a faith I could believe in. I heard a lot of words of compassion in Christianity that resonated with me, but I was disturbed and saddened by the hypocrisy I saw in those communities that did not welcome everyone into the light of their faith. I tried Judaism, Islam, Buddhism, Sikhism; I tried liberal and conservative; nothing fit. I learned so much from each faith, but the language was too foreign and didn't sync up quite right.

Then, almost as an afterthought, I went on a pilgrimage to Transylvania to where one version of Unitarianism had its origins. This journey was life altering. I felt as though whatever course was previously set had been lost, and I was drawn in an indistinct direction that said, "Go deeper." The true first steps of my pilgrim's quest started in a church in the city of Kolószvar in Romania. One of our guides, a woman named Chilla, was giving us a brief overview of

Transylvanian Unitarianism. She described it as a a a shared belief in the message of God's love. This message comes from a man named Jesus, who was a child of God just like you and me. His example, as reported by a good piece of literature called the Bible, is worth following. Transylvanian Unitarians have no stance on the afterlife, and their only statements about the nature of God are that God is one, not three, and that God is beneficent. When I heard this description, I felt as though I'd come home for the first time and discovered I'd been there all along. The guide had said that there was a religion that held my beliefs and reflected my values, and that it was the same tradition I had been a part of my whole life.

Our journey ended in a prison atop a hill in Deva, the place where a man named Francis David died. Francis David is the person generally credited with the founding of Unitarianism. He preached the unified nature of God and was eventually condemned to death for denying the Trinity and maintaining that freedom of conscience is a necessity and a human right. When I stood before the monument to his life in that tiny, grimy cell, his sufferings were suddenly so real to me that I began to cry. My fellow pilgrim, standing next to me, reached over and held my hand. The reality of the pain Jesus felt on the cross and the reality of the pain Michael Servetus felt when burning at the stake rushed into me, and I knew very clearly that human beings suffer. Sometimes people endure suffering for their values, sometimes for no reason, and no amount of love changes this. But sometimes suffering can be alleviated by making ourselves vulnerable to one another; by sharing the knowledge of our hurt, the carrying of our pain can be made easier. All the times I have felt alone, I have never really been alone because I have always been part of a community that I could tell, "I am hurting." My faith tradition acknowledged the bad along with the good by having a monument to our hero's miserable death and remarkable life. This knowledge healed all the ache of not knowing how to live with suffering. And realizing that Jesus, and his suffering, are really a deep part of my faith renewed me. As Chilla spoke in that church, I heard what I believed in language that was familiar. I finally felt at peace with being a Unitarian Universalist, knowing that I am also a Christian. I am part of a community that has roots in Christianity *and* steadfastly believes in my value as a queer person.

Consistently throughout my time as an activist, I have tried to spread the message that there are communities of faith that welcome and affirm queer folks. I have had positive experiences with communities of faith, so I spread the word as far and wide as I can that my church loves me for who I am and will love you not only in spite of your queerness but *because* of all of who you are. I believe with every fiber of my being that every person is loved. I can also see that not everyone knows it. The greatest depth of life's meaning, in my experience, comes from love; I want everyone to know that they are loved and that they have the ability to love. So I share my joy of the deep knowledge of the abiding love of God in everything I do. In my activism through BGLAD, the American Friends Service Committee, Food Not Bombs, AIDS Student Peer Educators at Newport High School (ASPEN), my music, and through my congregation, I try to help people know that religion doesn't have to be and shouldn't be painful but rather healing, joyous, and full of love. Also, by inviting people to my youth group meetings, I try to expose them to a truly loving and welcoming church community—within the walls of our youth room, there is no judgment. There is only support that, as far as I know, exists nowhere else.

The Unitarian Universalist Association forgets its guiding principles every time it cuts funding to youth ministries. I am surely a biased source if there ever was one, but I believe that the future of our movement is in those who have grown up in it. If we lose the youth, we lose it all.

Youth are capable of the most incredible things. Our youth ministries tell our young people that all people are valuable for who they are, from the day they are born to the day they die, and in any state in-between. Queer youth, especially, are vulnerable to the message that they are mistakes and don't fit into society, that they are not welcome in any community but the gay community. And God forbid you are trans—then nobody wants you. Except we do. Unitarian Universalist communities want to love and learn from queer youth of all kinds. At our worst, we reach out to queer folks as especially precious to our communities, which can be tokenizing. At our best, we make no assumptions about a person's sexual history or identity, we love and support the needs of individuals, and we fight for people's political rights and voice. The OWL program, for example, consistently includes people from every walk of life in its examples and recognizes the fact that sexuality comes in a variety of forms and expressions.

Only now can I look back and finally appreciate my Unitarian Universalist upbringing. I can see how my agnosticism has not been patronized as uncertainty but affirmed as faith. And I am grateful for the positivity I've been surrounded with about my body image and shape, my sexuality and sexual identity, and my general nerdiness (which I've never felt insecure about in the slightest). I can see how I've been shaped into a person who tries her hardest to treat everyone she meets with compassion. I am glad for the opportunities I've been given to explore my own faith and sexuality without judgment or fear. The boundaries set for me have been fair, the responsibilities reasonable, and the examples surrounding me exceptional.

Probably the best thing I've ever done, or at least the decision that has shaped me most, was taking middle-school OWL. OWL is based on the basic principle that all people are sexual beings their entire lives long. That means that everyone is in romantic, sexual, and/or platonic relationships as long as they are alive. That makes the demographics of the people included in the curriculum a lot wider than what our culture generally acknowledges.

OWL covers every possible way of being a sexual (or asexual) person, making no judgment, and teaching that life can be meaningful and rich when we acknowledge that sexuality is a part of our lives. I'll be honest; it was a little intense. Intense because I had to confront both my faith and my sexuality at the same time, while our larger culture refuses to acknowledge that those two things can go together positively. OWL lives up to our Unitarian Universalist value that all people have inherent worth and dignity by paying attention to the reality of many different expressions of sexuality. People I may not have wanted to think of as having sexual lives (the disabled, the elderly, my parents) are included in the curriculum. This inclusion has helped me grow on my journey to become less prejudiced against those groups and helped me reconcile attraction and love. I finally see clearly that faith and sexuality can be related, in a way that makes sense of my identity and makes my relationships more meaningful.

For the past year, I've dated a young man. My interest in him came out of the blue; I had convinced myself and those closest to me that I was attracted only to women. As I discovered, love is not concerned with who you think you are attracted to. He and I met through our church youth group and since have become very close. Being in a relationship with him has enriched my spiritual and intellectual life and helped me learn the real meaning of loving another and loving myself. He has challenged me and my values, and kept me strong in the foundation of my principles in ways I never would have imagined. And without OWL, I might never have recognized that I was both physically and emotionally attracted to him. I never would have been able to act on those feelings. My feelings put me at risk of rejection from those I had come out to as woman-identified, and they forced me to re-examine the particulars of my queer identity. But because I was able to see that love and attraction could fit together to make the most beautiful masterpiece of connection, I have had a fulfilling and deeply meaningful friendship and romantic relationship for the past year that I otherwise would have ignored.

OWL will be a source of wisdom throughout my entire life, I'm sure. I am so proud to be a Unitarian Universalist because of the way I have been raised. I love this tradition more and more each day as I see its gifts unfold.

I also believe that, if you truly love something, you help it grow. I see a lot more work for us to do, and I am going to hold us accountable for doing it. So often I am frustrated by Unitarian Universalists who wonder where all the young adults are. We have to reach out to them. I am confident we already have the message they want to hear: You are valuable, you are loved, you are not alone, and our commitment is to support you as you grow more fully into yourself. Once youth come to our congregations, we also must listen to them. For people to be a part of a community, they must know that their needs will be met and that they can serve the needs of the community. We must provide this promise to everyone interested in Unitarian Universalism. We have the message; we just lack the gusto to get it out there. We must stop trying to be perfect and acknowledge that we are doing many things right. New members who love our message can help us see what we don't and how to adjust.

Another way we need to be more welcoming is to confront the lingering bitterness toward, and fear of, Christianity that many members in our congregations carry. Many Unitarian Universalists refuse to acknowledge their prejudice against Christians. They deny our roots in Christianity. We will not be truly welcoming and affirming of everyone until we stand face to face with our Christophobia and begin to heal the deep wounds "traditional" religious teachings have inflicted on our souls.

How tragic that we have such beautiful communities and a message that could heal this world, but we hide it under a bushel. The more actively we share the joy of our message, the more we will see the world heal before our eyes. So many queer people could find a faith home among us and heal their painful wounds from other encounters with religion. I have seen how the joy of an affirming faith can be transformational. New life can be brought to people who have given up.

Faith communities are special because they can tell you that you are significant for something no other community can name, the spark of the Universe within you, the fact that you are here and alive and loved. Through Unitarian Universalism, I have learned that these things are what make me—and every person—remarkable.

—◦—

ROWAN McDOWELL THOMPSON *is a seventeen-year-old senior in high school in Bellevue, Washington. Her home congregation is East Shore Unitarian Church near Seattle, which she has attended for twelve years. A European-American who has lived her whole life in the Pacific Northwest, Rowan is a peer sex-educator for her school district, a cellist, and a water polo player.*

Glossary

Ally. An individual who demonstrates a belief in equal rights and access for people who are lesbian, gay, bisexual, transgender, intersex, queer, and or genderqueer.

Bisexual. Someone who identifies their sexuality as encompassing the potential to be attracted to members of both the "same" sex and the "opposite" sex.

Butch. A term used to describe someone seen as exhibiting stereotypically masculine appearance, behavior, attitudes, particularly in reference to women. The value judgment associated with this term often differs depending on who uses it.

Closet. A shorthand term for "being in the closet," which means being invisible or hiding one's LGBTQ identity. Debate exists within the LGBTQ community whether it is appropriate to bring someone out of the closet without their consent, such as elected leaders who vote for anti-gay legislation while remaining closeted as LGBTQ.

Coming out. A shorthand phrase for "coming out of the closet," used to describe the process most LGBTQ people experience as they grow in awareness of their sexual orientation/gender identity. Coming out may be private or public. Typically, it is an ongoing process of deepening self-knowledge. Non-gay family, friends, allies, and others may also experience feeling closeted and coming out as part of their relationship to LGBTQ people. Someone may be "outed" involuntarily by another person, whether or not the attribution is true; for example, although women comprise only 14 percent of the military, 48 percent of discharges under Don't Ask, Don't Tell have been of women, often due to third-party accusations.

Domestic Partner Benefits (DPBs). One way employers attempt to equalize the significant difference in financial benefits available to married heterosexuals compared with other employees. More than 56 percent of *Fortune* 500 companies currently provide DPBs to their employees, as do hundreds of cities, businesses, and nonprofits.

Don't Ask, Don't Tell (DADT). The name commonly used for 1993 legislation that created a policy across the U.S. Armed Forces that allowed lesbian, gay, and bisexual service members to remain in the military only if they did not reveal their sexual orientation. More than 14 thousand service members were discharged between 1993 and 2011 under Don't Ask, Don't Tell, including a number who assert they are not gay or lesbian and others who were outed by their commanders. Congress voted to repeal DADT in December 2010.

FTM (female-to-male). A term used to identify someone who was identified at birth as female but who self-identifies as male/masculine. Some transgender people may find the label FTM offensive because it may imply that they did not initially identify themselves as male or masculine.

Femme. A term used to describe someone who is seen as exhibiting stereotypically feminine appearance, behavior, and attitudes. In reference to men, the term is often equated with weakness or lack of "manliness."

Gay. Historically, the most frequently used term identifying people who have a same-sex orientation and/or the community they are assumed to be part of ("the gay community"). Usage is complicated by research that shows people associate the term almost exclusively with men and recognition that gender identity is distinct from sexual orientation.

Genderqueer. A term used by some to identify themselves in opposition to the socially constructed standards of masculinity and femininity that provide the basis for negative stereotypes and/or discrimination against LGBTQI people.

Heterosexual. Someone who identifies as exclusively attracted to members of the "opposite" sex.

Heterosexism. The cultural bias that everyone is, should be, or wants to be heterosexual, just as *sexism* denotes the value placed on maleness.

Homophobe. A person who is fearful of homosexuals. At one time, homophobia, also called *homosexual panic*, was accepted as part of a legal defense of physical, verbal, and emotional abuse of people who are LGBTQ.

Homosexual. Someone who identifies as primarily or exclusively attracted to others of the same sex. Others may willfully or ignorantly identify someone as homosexual based on cultural stereotypes, irrespective of the target's identity.

Intersex. A broad term used for a spectrum of conditions in which a person is born with a reproductive or sexual anatomy and/or genetics that don't fit the normative definition of biologically male or female.

Interweave: Unitarian Universalists for LGBT Concerns. A nonprofit membership organization that complements the Unitarian Universalist Association's efforts on behalf of LGBTQ equality.

Lesbian. A term that refers to women who identify as attracted erotically to women; others may willfully or ignorantly identify someone as lesbian based on cultural stereotypes, irrespective of the target's identity. A significant number of women who love women prefer *gay* or terms such as *woman-identified* rather than *lesbian*.

MTF (male-to-female). A term used to identify someone who was identified as male at birth but who identifies as female/feminine. Some transgender people may find the label offensive because it may imply that they did not initially identify themselves as female or feminine.

Our Whole Lives (OWL). A sexuality education curriculum offered by the Unitarian Universalist Association as part of youth and adult religious education. OWL affirms all sexual orientations and gender identities and promotes a holistic view of sexuality.

Queer. A term that may refer to any sexual orientation and/or gender identity or expression that does not conform to societal norms. The word *queer* is considered controversial and even offensive by some, especially older LGBTQ people. Many younger LGBTQ people have re-claimed the term as a means of self-empowerment.

Questioning. A relatively new term for those who prefer not to identify as straight, lesbian, gay, bisexual, or transgender. It may refer to someone who is exploring their identity, without feeling drawn to a specific self-description.

Sex Reassignment Surgery (SRS). Surgery or surgeries some undergo as part of their gender transition. Medical practitioners generally require SRS clients to undergo extensive psychological counseling and present in their self-identified gender for a year prior to surgery.

Sexual orientation/sexual identity. A term used to describe which sex(es) or gender(s) a person is attracted to erotically. Decades of research on whether one's sexuality is innate or learned supports an interaction of nature and nurture. The term *sexual preference* is not considered appropriate because it implies that one's orientation is chosen. Sexual orientation is also often used as shorthand for *gay*. For example, corporate non-discrimination policies that include "sexual orientation" are rarely interpreted as designed to protect straight employees. The term *sexual identity* avoids this confusion and de-emphasizes the concept of choice. While language referring to someone's sexual orientation or identity tends to reflect binary categories like gay or straight, most people fall somewhere along a continuum ranging from exclusively heterosexual to exclusively homosexual.

Sexuality and Our Faith. The religious curriculum series that complements *Our Whole Lives* in Unitarian Universalist and United Church of Christ settings.

Straight. A term used to describe heterosexuals, with historical references to "straight arrow" or correctly aligned rather than bent or out of alignment. Just as gay people may be lumped together as "gays," nongay people may be lumped together as "straights" in preference to the more clinical terms, *homosexuals* and *heterosexuals*.

Stonewall Riot. A highly publicized instance of resistance to a police raid on a gay bar, the Stonewall Inn, in New York

City on June 28, 1969. It is often cited as the beginning of the modern gay rights movement.

Transgender. A term used to describe someone who identifies as being outside attitudes, behavior, and/or appearances that normatively define gender as masculine or feminine. Someone may identify as transgender without desiring surgery, a name change, or other measures typically linked with transgender identity.

Transitioning. The process of socially or physically changing one's gender to align with one's biological or psychological identity. This process can include any or all of the following: name change, surgery, hormone replacement therapy, and other expressions of one's gender such as dress and hair.

Transsexual. A term used to describe someone who experiences intense, persistent, long-term discomfort with their body and self-image due to awareness that their apparent biological sex does not match their self-identification. People who identify as transsexual may be preoperative or postoperative or may not desire surgery, a name change, or other measures typically linked with a transsexual identity.

Welcoming Congregation. A program established by the Unitarian Universalist Association in 1990 to support congregations in increasing awareness of the experiences and concerns of LGBTQ people and their allies.

Resources

The Advocate. An LGBT bi-monthly newsmagazine. Established in 1967, it is the oldest ongoing LGBT publication in the United States. Coverage includes international news and events. www.advocate.com

Michelle Bates Deakin. *Gay Marriage, Real Life: Ten Stories of Love and Family.* Boston: Skinner House Books, 2005. Based on interviews with couples and family members across the country, old and young, accepted and alienated, these telling stories capture the powerful and dramatic effect that the legalization of same-sex marriage is having on our families and society.

Rob Eichberg. *Coming Out: An Act of Love.* New York: Dutton, 1990. Written by a psychologist and cofounder of a self-empowerment movement, The Experience.

John D'Emilio. *The World Turned: Essays on Gay History, Politics, and Culture.* Durham, NC: Duke University Press,

2002. A well-researched academic activist's view of "gay" history.

John Gallagher and Chris Bull. *Perfect Enemies: The Battle Between the Religious Right and the Gay Movement*. New York: Madison Books, 1996. An insightful analysis of the symbiotic relationship between "Religious Right" and "Gay Movement" activists.

Jamison Green. *Becoming a Visible Man*. Nashville, TN: Vanderbilt University Press, 2004. A first-person account, supported by research, on the experiences of being transgender.

Lani Ka'ahumanu and Loraine Hutchins, eds. *Bi Any Other Name: Bisexual People Speak Out*. Boston, MA: Alyson Books, 1991. A collection of first-person essays about the experiences of being bisexual.

David Kinnaman and Gabe Lyons. *Unchristian: What a New Generation Really Thinks About Christianity . . . and Why It Matters*. Grand Rapids, MI: Baker Books, 2007. Written by evangelical Christians, the president of the Barna Group and founder of the Fermi Project, respectively. Offers a hard look at why religion turns off so many in the GenX and millennial age groups.

Debra Kolodny. *Blessed Bi Spirit*. New York: Continuum International Publishing, 2000. Essays that explore the spiritual struggles of and affirm bisexual people of faith in a culture focused on a heterosexual/homosexual binary.

Brian McNaught. *Gay Issues in the Workplace*. New York: St. Martin's Press, 1993. The foundational book on workplace equity for LGBT employees. McNaught is known as the "godfather of gay rights."

Robyn Ochs and Sarah E. Rowley. *Getting Bi: Voices of Bisexuals Around the World*. Boston: Bisexual Resource Center, 2009. Essays from an international assemblage of bisexual women and men that define bisexuality, community, and politics. Offers resources for bi and non-bi people.

Dan Savage and Terry Miller, eds. *It Gets Better: Coming Out, Overcoming Bullying, and Creating a Life Worth Living*. New York: Dutton Adult, 2011. A collection of essays by LGBTQ people on their their experiences of surviving anti-gay bullying.

Websites

At the time of printing, these were current website addresses for major LGBTQ-supportive organizations.

American Institute of Bisexuality. The Institute provides historical background and research on bisexuality, including the pioneering work of Alfred Kinsey (the Kinsey Scale) and Fritz Klein (Klein Sexual Orientation Grid). **www.bisexual.org**

American Psychological Association (APA). The APA has been a leader in research, teaching, and advocacy for LGBTQ equality, removing homosexuality from the *Diag-*

nostic and Statistical Manual of Mental Disorders (DSM) in 1973. The APA has a Division on the Psychological Study of Lesbian and Gay Issues and there is an APA Office of LGBT Concerns in Washington, D.C. **www.apa.org**

Gay and Lesbian Alliance Against Defamation (GLAAD). A nonprofit that was established in 1985 in response to negative stereotyping of gay men in media coverage of AIDS. GLAAD provides a Media Reference Guide, monitors media depictions of LGBTQ people, educates leaders on effective presentations and non-stereotypic portrayals, and gives awards for positive media visibility of gay people. **www.glaad.org**

Gay, Lesbian and Straight Education Network (GLSEN). A nonprofit founded in 1990 that supports, educates, and advocates on behalf of LGBTQ students and faculty. Projects include the Safe Space Campaign, National School Climate Survey, Gay Student Associations (GSAs), and anti-bullying programs. **www.glsen.org**

Human Rights Campaign (HRC). The largest LGBTQ political action committee in the United States. The HRC also supports major projects on workplace discrimination, LGBTQ rights, and religion. **www.hrc.org**

International Lesbian, Gay, Bisexual, Trans, and Intersex Association (ILGA). An international organization that brings together hundreds of lesbian and gay groups from around the world and campaigns for LGBTI rights on the international human rights and civil rights scene. Based in Belgium, the ILGA is represented in around 110 countries across the world. Website contains information on LGBT laws and rights by country. **www.ilga.org**

International Gay and Lesbian Human Rights Commission (IGLHRC). A leading international organization dedicated to human rights advocacy on behalf of people who experience discrimination or abuse on the basis of their actual or perceived sexual orientation, gender identity, or expression. Contains LGBTQ news by country. **www.iglghc.org**

Interweave: Unitarian Universalists for Lesbian, Gay, Bisexual and Transgender Concerns. A nonprofit 501 organization that complements the Unitarian Universalist Association's efforts on behalf of LGBTQ equality. Interweave publishes a quarterly newsletter and holds a semiannual conference. **www.interweave.org**

It Gets Better **Campaign.** A YouTube campaign started on September 21, 2010, by gay blogger Dan Savage, after a spate of gay teen suicides in the United States. The website hosts more than 10,000 videos offering a message of hope from a wide variety of people, including rural teens, President Barack Obama, Secretary of State Hillary Clinton, actor Colin Farrell, Project Runway host Tim Gunn, TV star Ellen DeGeneres, and financial advisor Suze Orman. Since its inception, *It Gets Better* has recorded more than 30 million views. **www.itgetsbetter.org**

National Center for Lesbian Rights (NCLR). Founded in 1977 in San Francisco as the Lesbian Rights Project of Equal Rights Advocates, the NCLR advances the legal and human rights of LGBTQ people and their families across the United States. **www.nclrights.org**

National Gay and Lesbian Task Force (NGLTF). The mission of the NGLTF is to build the grassroots power of the LGBT community by training activists, equipping state and local organizations with the skills to organize broad-based campaigns for policy change at local and national levels, and building the organizational capacity of the LGBT movement. The NGLTF Policy Institute, the movement's premier think tank, provides research and policy analysis to support the struggle for LGBT equality. **www.thetaskforce.org**

National Lesbian and Gay Journalists Association (NLGJA). The oldest and largest association of professional journalists, writers, students, and allies with expertise on LGBTQ issues in the United States. NLGJA also publishes a stylebook of language appropriate for describing LGBTQ individuals and events in the media. **www.nlgja.org**

Out and Equal Workplace Advocates. A nonprofit membership association of individuals and employers promoting workplace equality for LGBTQ people. Offers training, online publications, career postings open to members, and an annual conference. **www.outandequal.org**

Parents, Friends, and Family for Lesbians and Gays (PFLAG). A nonprofit initially established in 1973 as an educational and support service for parents of lesbian and gay children. PFLAG has evolved into advocacy work on behalf of LGBTQ issues and has many LGBTQ people among its 200 thousand members. **www.pflag.org**

Services and Advocacy for LGBT Elders (SAGE). A nonprofit association established in 1978 that provides education, services, and advocacy for older people who are LGBT and for service providers. **www.sageusa.org**

Unitarian Universalist Association (UUA). An association of non-creedal, liberal religious congregations in the United States and Canada. In 1970, the UUA was one of two religious associations to pass membership-supported resolutions opposing discrimination on the basis of sexual orientation (the other was the United Church of Christ). Since 1975, the UUA has supported LGBTQ rights through internal and external education, support, and advocacy with programs such as the Welcoming Congregation program. *Standing on the Side of Love* is a UUA-sponsored initiative that promotes marriage equality and immigration reform. www.uua.org, **www.standingonthesideoflove.org**

Wikipedia. An open source (user-written, edited, and monitored) encyclopedic online resource that covers myriad issues related to LGBTQ identity and concerns, among others. **www.wikipedia.org**